MILITARY COMMISSIONS ACT OF 2006: ANALYSES

For permission to use material from this book please contact us:
Telephone 631-231-7269; Fax 631-231-8175
Web Site: http://www.novapublishers.com

NOTICE TO THE READER

LIBRARY OF CONGRESS CATALOGING-IN-PUBLICATION DATA

Elsea, Jennifer
Military Commissions Act of 2006 : analyses / Jennifer K. Elsea.
p. cm.
ISBN 978-1-60456-535-5(softcover)
1.Military courts—United States.2.Prisoners of war—Legal Status, laws, etc.3.Detention of prisoners—United States.4. United States. Military commissions Act of 2006. I. Title.
KF7661.E473 2008
343.73'0143—dc22 2008011214

Published by Nova Science Publishers, Inc. ≃ New York

CONTENTS

PREFACE

This book provides a background and analysis comparing military commissions as envisioned under the MCA to the rules that had been established by the Department of Defense (DOD) for military commissions and to general military courts-martial conducted under the UCMJ. After reviewing the history of the implementation of military commissions in the "global war on terrorism," this book provides an overview of the procedural safeguards provided in the MCA. This book identifies pending legislation, including H.R. 267, H.R. 1585, H.R. 2543, H.R. 2826, S. 1547, S. 1548, H.R. 1416, S. 1876, S. 185, S. 576, S.447, H.R. 1415 and H.R. 2710. Finally, the book provides two tables comparing the MCA with regulations that had been issued by the Department of Defense pursuant to the President's Military Order with standard procedures for general courts-martial under the Manual for Courts-Martial. The first table describes the composition and powers of the military tribunals, as well as their jurisdiction. The second chart compares procedural safeguards required by the MCA with those that had been incorporated in the DOD regulations and the established procedures in courts-martial.

THE MILITARY COMMISSIONS ACT OF 2006: ANALYSIS OF PROCEDURAL RULES AND COMPARISON WITH PREVIOUS DOD RULES AND THE UNIFORM CODE OF MILITARY JUSTICE*

SUMMARY

On November 13, 2001, President Bush issued a Military Order (M.O.) pertaining to the detention, treatment, and trial of certain non-citizens in the war against terrorism. Military commissions pursuant to the M.O. began in November 2004 against four persons declared eligible for trial, but proceedings were suspended after a federal district court found that one of the defendants could not be tried under the rules established by the Department of Defense (DOD). The D.C. Circuit Court of Appeals reversed that decision in *Rumsfeld v. Hamdan*, but the Supreme Court granted review and reversed the decision of the Court of Appeals. To permit military commissions to go forward, Congress approved the Military Commissions Act of 2006 (MCA), conferring authority to promulgate rules that depart from the strictures of the Uniform Code of Military Justice (UCMJ) and possibly U.S. international obligations. The Department of Defense published regulations to govern military commissions pursuant to the MCA.

---

* Excerpted from CRS Report RL33688. Updated September 27, 2007.

The Court of Military Commissions Review (CMCR), created by the MCA, issued its first decision on September 24, 2007, reversing a dismissal of charges based on lack of jurisdiction and ordering the military judge to determine whether the accused is an "unlawful enemy combatant" subject to the military commission's jurisdiction. The CMCR rejected the government's argument that the determination by a Combatant Status Review Tribunal (CSRT) that a detainee is an "enemy combatant" was a sufficient basis for jurisdiction, but also rejected the military judge's finding that the military commission was not empowered to make the appropriate determination.

This book provides a background and analysis comparing military commissions as envisioned under the MCA to the rules that had been established by the Department of Defense (DOD) for military commissions and to general military courts-martial conducted under the UCMJ. After reviewing the history of the implementation of military commissions in the "global war on terrorism," the report provides an overview of the procedural safeguards provided in the MCA. The report identifies pending legislation, including H.R. 267, H.R. 1585, H.R. 2543, H.R. 2826, S. 1547, S. 1548, H.R. 1416, S. 1876, S. 185, S. 576, S.447, H.R. 1415 and H.R. 2710. Finally, the report provides two tables comparing the MCA with regulations that had been issued by the Department of Defense pursuant to the President's Military Order with standard procedures for general courts-martial under the Manual for Courts-Martial. The first table describes the composition and powers of the military tribunals, as well as their jurisdiction. The second chart, which compares procedural safeguards required by the MCA with those that had been incorporated in the DOD regulations and the established procedures in courts-martial, follows the same order and format used in CRS Report RL31262, *Selected Procedural Safeguards in Federal, Military, and International Courts*, to facilitate comparison with safeguards provided in federal court and international criminal tribunals.

Chapter 1

INTRODUCTION

Rasul v. Bush, issued by the U.S. Supreme Court at the end of its 2003-2004 term, clarified that U.S. courts do have jurisdiction to hear petitions for habeas corpus on behalf of the approximately 550 persons then detained at the U.S. Naval Station in Guantanamo Bay, Cuba, in connection with the war against terrorism,[1] establishing a role for federal courts to play in determining the validity of the military commissions convened pursuant to President Bush's Military Order (M.O.) of November 13, 2001.[2] After dozens of petitions for habeas corpus were filed in the federal District Court for the District of Columbia, Congress passed the Detainee Treatment Act of 2005 (DTA),[3] revoking federal court jurisdiction over habeas claims, at least with respect to those not already pending, and creating jurisdiction in the Court of Appeals for the District of Columbia Circuit to hear appeals of final decisions of military commissions. The Supreme Court, in *Hamdan v. Rumsfeld*,[4] overturned a decision by the D.C. Circuit that had upheld the military commissions, holding instead that although Congress has authorized the use of military commissions, such commissions must follow procedural rules as similar as possible to courts-martial proceedings, in compliance with the Uniform Code of Military Justice (UCMJ).[5] In response, Congress passed the Military Commissions Act of 2006 (MCA)[6] to authorize military commissions and establish procedural rules that are modeled after, but depart from in some significant ways, the UCMJ.

The Department of Defense has issued regulations for the conduct of military commissions pursuant to the MCA.[7] One detainee, David Matthew Hicks of Australia, was convicted of material support to terrorism pursuant to a plea agreement. Trials began for two other defendants, but were halted after the military judges dismissed charges based on lack of jurisdiction, finding in both cases that the defendants had not properly been found to be "unlawful enemy combatants." The prosecutors appealed the cases to the Court of Military Commissions Review (CMCR), which reversed the dismissal of charges in one case and remanded it to the military commission for a determination of whether the accused is an "unlawful enemy combatant."[8] The CMCR decision rejected the government's contention that the determination by a Combatant Status Review Tribunal (CSRT) that a detainee is an "enemy combatant" was a sufficient basis for jurisdiction, but also rejected the military judge's finding that the military commission was not itself empowered to make the appropriate determination.

Military Commissions: General Background

Military commissions are courts usually set up by military commanders in the field to try persons accused of certain offenses during war.[9] Past military commissions trying enemy belligerents for war crimes directly applied the international law of war, without recourse to domestic criminal statutes, unless such statutes were declaratory of international law.[10] Historically, military commissions have applied the same set of procedural rules that applied in courts-martial.[11] By statute, military tribunals may be used to try "offenders or offenses designated by statute or the law of war."[12] Although the Supreme Court long ago stated that charges of violations of the law of war tried before military commissions need not be as exact as those brought before regular courts,[13] it is unclear whether the current Court would adopt that proposition or look more closely to precedent.

The President's Military Order establishing military commissions to try suspected terrorists was the focus of intense debate both at home and abroad. Critics argued that the tribunals could violate any rights the accused may have under the Constitution as well as their rights under international law, thereby undercutting the legitimacy of any verdicts rendered by the tribunals. The Administration established rules prescribing detailed procedural safeguards for the tribunals in Military Commission Order No. 1 ("M.C.O. No. 1"), issued in March 2002 and amended in 2005.[14] These rules were praised as a significant improvement over what might have been permitted under the language of the M.O., but some continued to argue that the enhancements did not go far enough and called for the checks and balances of a separate rule-making authority and an independent appellate process.[15] Critics also noted that the rules did not address the issue of indefinite detention without charge, as appeared to be possible under the original M.O.,[16] or that the Department of Defense may continue to detain persons who have been cleared by a military commission.[17] The Pentagon has reportedly stated that its Inspector General (IG) looked into allegations, made by military lawyers assigned as prosecutors to the military commissions, that the proceedings are rigged to obtain convictions, but the IG did not substantiate the charges.[18]

President Bush determined that twenty of the detainees at the U.S. Naval Station in Guantánamo Bay were subject to the M.O., and 10 were subsequently charged for trial before military commissions.[19]

Hamdan v. Rumsfeld

Salim Ahmed Hamdan was captured in Afghanistan and charged with conspiracy for having allegedly worked for Osama Bin Laden.[20] He challenged the lawfulness of the military commission under the UCMJ[21] and claimed the right to be treated as a prisoner of war under the Geneva Conventions.[22] A ruling in his favor at the district court was reversed by the D.C. Circuit Court of Appeals, which, while rejecting the government's argument that the federal courts had no jurisdiction to interfere in ongoing commission proceedings, agreed with the government that the Geneva Conventions are not judicially enforceable;[23] that even if they were, Hamdan was not entitled to their protections; and that in any event, the military commission would qualify as a "competent tribunal" for challenging the petitioner's non-POW status. The appellate court did not accept the government's argument that the President has inherent authority to create military commissions without any authorization from Congress, but found such authority in the Authorization to Use Military Force (AUMF),[24] read together with UCMJ arts. 21 and 36.[25]

The Supreme Court granted review and reversed. Before reaching the merits of the case, the Supreme Court dispensed with the government's argument that Congress had, by passing the Detainee Treatment Act of 2005 (DTA),[26] stripped the Court of its jurisdiction to review habeas corpus challenges by or on behalf of Guantanamo detainees whose petitions had already been filed.[27] In addition, regardless of whether the Geneva Conventions provide rights that are enforceable in Article III courts, the Court found that Congress, by incorporating the "law of war" into UCMJ art. 21,[28] brought the Geneva Conventions within the scope of law to be applied by courts.[29] Further, the Court found that, at the very least, Common Article 3 of the Geneva Conventions applies, even to members of al Qaeda, according to them a minimum baseline of protections, including protection from the "passing of sentences and the carrying out of executions without previous judgment pronounced by a regularly constituted court, affording all the judicial guarantees which are recognized as indispensable by civilized peoples."[30]

The Court concluded that, although Common Article 3 "obviously tolerates a great degree of flexibility in trying individuals captured during armed conflict" and that "its requirements are general ones, crafted to accommodate a wide variety of legal systems," the military commissions under M.C.O. No. 1 did not meet these criteria. In particular, the military commissions were not "regularly constituted" because they deviated too far, in the Court's view, from the rules that apply to courts-martial, without a satisfactory explanation of the need for such deviation.[31] Justice Scalia, joined by Justices Thomas and Alito, dissented, arguing that the DTA should be interpreted to preclude the Court's review.

Chapter 2

THE MILITARY COMMISSIONS ACT OF 2006

In response to the *Hamdan* decision, Congress enacted the Military Commissions Act of 2006 ("MCA") to grant the President express authority to convene military commissions to prosecute those fitting the definition under the MCA of "alien unlawful enemy combatants." The MCA eliminates the requirement for military commissions to conform to either of the two uniformity requirements in article 36, UCMJ. Instead, it establishes a new chapter 47A in title 10, U.S. Code and excepts military commissions under the new chapter from the requirements in article 36.[32] It provides that the UCMJ "does not, by its terms, apply to trial by military commissions except as specifically provided in this chapter." While declaring that the new chapter is "based upon the procedures for trial by general courts-martial under [the UCMJ]," it establishes that "[t]he judicial construction and application of [the UCMJ] are not binding on military commissions established under this chapter."[33] It expressly exempts the new military commission from UCMJ articles 10 (speedy trial), 31 (self-incrimination warnings) and 32 (pretrial investigations), and amends articles 21, 28, 48, 50(a), 104, and 106 of the UCMJ to except military commissions under the new chapter.[34] Other provisions of the UCMJ are to apply to trial by military commissions under the new chapter only to the extent provided therein.[35]

JURISDICTION

The President's M.O. was initially criticized by some as overly broad in its assertion of jurisdiction, because it could be interpreted to cover non-citizens who had no connection with Al Qaeda or the terrorist attacks of September 11, 2001, as well as offenders or offenses not triable by military commission pursuant to statute or the law of war.[36] A person subject to the M.O. was amenable to detention and possible trial by military tribunal for violations of the law of war and "other applicable law."[37]

M.C.O. No. 1 established that commissions may be convened to try aliens designated by the President as subject to the M.O., whether captured overseas or on U.S. territory, for violations of the law of war and "all other offenses triable by military commissions." The MCA largely validates the President's jurisdictional scheme for military commissions.

Personal Jurisdiction

While many observers agreed that the President is authorized by statute to convene military commissions in the "Global War on Terrorism," some believed the President's constitutional and statutory authority to establish such tribunals does not extend beyond Congress' authorization to use armed force in response to the attacks.[38] Under a literal interpretation of the M.O., however, the President could designate as subject to the order any non-citizen he believed had ever engaged in any activity related to international terrorism, no matter when or where these acts took place.

The M.O. was not cited for the authority to detain; instead, the Department of Defense asserted its authority to be grounded in the law of war, which permits belligerents to kill or capture and detain enemy combatants. The Department of Defense defined "enemy combatant" to mean "an individual who was part of or supporting Taliban or al Qaeda forces, or associated forces that are engaged in hostilities against the United States or its coalition partners," including "any person who has committed a belligerent act or has directly supported hostilities in aid of enemy armed forces."[39]

The MCA applies a somewhat broader definition for "unlawful enemy combatant," which includes

> (i) a person who has engaged in hostilities or who has purposefully and materially supported hostilities against the United States or its co-belligerents who is not a lawful enemy combatant (including a person who is part of the Taliban, al Qaeda, or associated forces); or
>
> (ii) a person who, before, on, or after the date of the enactment of the Military Commissions Act of 2006, has been determined to be an unlawful enemy combatant by a Combatant Status Review Tribunal or another competent tribunal established under the authority of the President or the Secretary of Defense.[40]

Thus, persons who do not directly participate in hostilities, but "purposefully and materially" support hostilities, are subject to treatment as an "unlawful enemy combatant" under the MCA. Citizens who fit the definition of "unlawful enemy combatant" are not amenable to trial by military commission under the MCA, but may be subject to detention.

The MCA does not define "hostilities" or explain what conduct amounts to "supporting hostilities." To the extent that the jurisdiction is interpreted to include conduct that falls outside the accepted definition of participation in an armed conflict, the MCA might run afoul of the courts' historical aversion to trying civilians before military tribunal when other courts are available.[41] It is unclear whether this principle would apply to aliens captured and detained overseas, but the MCA does not appear to exempt from military jurisdiction permanent resident aliens captured in the United States who might otherwise meet the definition of "unlawful enemy combatant." It is generally accepted that aliens within the United States are entitled to the same protections in criminal trials that apply to U.S. citizens. Therefore, to subject persons to trial by military commission who do not meet the exception carved out by the Supreme Court in *ex parte Quirin*[42] for unlawful belligerents, to the extent such persons enjoy constitutional protections, would likely raise significant constitutional questions.

The MCA did not specifically identify who makes the determination that defendants meet the definition of "unlawful enemy combatant." The government sought to establish jurisdiction based on the determinations of Combatant Status Review Tribunals (CSRTs), set up by the Pentagon to determine the status of detainees using procedures similar to those the Army uses to determine POW status during traditional wars.[43] The CSRTs, however, are not empowered to determine whether the enemy combatants are unlawful or lawful, which recently led two military commission judges to hold that CSRT determinations are inadequate to form the basis for the jurisdiction of military commissions.[44] One of the judges determined that the military commission itself is not competent to make the determination, while the other judge appears to have determined that the government's allegations did not set forth sufficient facts to conclude that the defendant, Salim Hamdan, was an unlawful enemy combatant.[45] The Court of Military Commission Review (CMCR) reversed the dismissal in the first case.[46] While it agreed that the CSRT determinations are insufficient by themselves to establish jurisdiction, it found the military judge erred in declaring that the status determination had to be made by a competent tribunal other than the military commission itself.

In denying the government's request to find that CSRT determinations are sufficient to establish jurisdiction over the accused, the CMCR interpreted the MCA to require more than establishing membership in Al Qaeda or the Taliban. The CMCR found

> no support for [the government's] claim that Congress, through the M.C.A., created a "comprehensive system" which sought to embrace and adopt all prior C.S.R.T. determinations that resulted in "enemy combatant" status assignments, and summarily

> turn those designations into findings that persons so labeled could also properly be considered "unlawful enemy combatants." Similarly, we find no support for [the government's] position regarding the parenthetical language contained in § 948a(1)(A)(i) of the M.C.A. — "including a person who is part of the Taliban, al Qaeda, or associated forces." We do not read this language as declaring that a member of the Taliban, al Qaeda, or associated forces is *per se* an "unlawful enemy combatant" for purposes of exercising criminal jurisdiction before a military commission. We read the parenthetical comment as simply elaborating upon the sentence immediately preceding it. That is, that a member of the Taliban, al Qaeda, or associated forces who has engaged in hostilities or who has purposefully and materially supported hostilities against the United States or its co-belligerents will also qualify as an "unlawful enemy combatant" under the M.C.A. (emphasis added [by the court]).[47]

The CMCR further explained that executive branch memoranda defining "enemy combatant" status were implemented solely for purposes of continued detention of personnel captured during hostilities and applicability of the Geneva Conventions. By contrast,

> Congress in the M.C.A. was carefully and deliberately defining status for the express purpose of specifying the in personam criminal jurisdiction of military commission trials. In defining what was clearly intended to be limited jurisdiction, Congress also prescribed serious criminal sanctions for those members of this select group who were ultimately convicted by military commissions.[48]

Further, because detainees could not have known when their CSRT reviews were taking place that the determination could subject them to the jurisdiction of a military commission, the CMCR suggested that the use of CSRT determinations to establish jurisdiction would undermine Congress's intent that military commissions operate as "regularly constituted court[s], affording all the necessary 'judicial guarantees which are recognized as indispensable by civilized peoples' for purposes of Common Article 3 of the Geneva Conventions."[49]

As a consequence of the decision, the Department of Defense will not have to institute new status tribunals, but the prosecution has the burden of proving jurisdiction over each person charged for trial by a military commission.

Subject-Matter Jurisdiction

The MCA provides jurisdiction to military commissions over "any offense made punishable by this chapter or the law of war when committed by an alien unlawful enemy combatant...."[50] Crimes to be triable by military commission are defined in subchapter VII (10 U.S.C. §§ 950p - 950w). Offenses include the following: murder of protected persons; attacking civilians, civilian objects, or protected property; pillaging; denying quarter; taking hostages; employing poison or similar weapons; using protected persons or property as shields; torture, cruel or inhuman treatment; intentionally causing serious bodily injury; mutilating or maiming; murder in violation of the law of war; destruction of property in violation of the law of war; using treachery or perfidy; improperly using a flag of truce or distinctive emblem; intentionally mistreating a dead body; rape; sexual assault or abuse; hijacking or hazarding a vessel or aircraft; terrorism; providing material support for terrorism; wrongfully aiding the enemy; spying; contempt; perjury and obstruction of justice. 10 U.S.C. § 950v. Conspiracy (§ 950v(b)(28)), attempts (§ 950t), and solicitation (§ 950u) to commit the defined acts are also punishable.

Military commissions under M.C.O. No. 1 were to have jurisdiction over crimes listed in M.C.I. No. 2, Crimes and Elements for Trials by Military Commission,[51] which appears to have served as a basis for the MCA list. The list of crimes in M.C.I. No. 2 was not meant to be exhaustive. Rather, it was intended as an illustration of acts punishable under the law of war[52] or triable by military commissions,[53] but did not permit trial for *ex post facto* crimes.[54]

Although many of the crimes defined in the MCA seem to be well-established offenses against the law of war, at least in the context of an international armed conflict,[55] a court might conclude that some of the listed crimes are new. For example, a plurality of the Supreme Court in *Hamdan* agreed that conspiracy is not a war crime under the traditional law of war.[56] The crime of "murder in violation of the law of war," which punishes persons who, as unprivileged belligerents, commit hostile acts that result in the death of any persons, including lawful combatants, may also be new. While it appears to be well-established that a civilian who kills a lawful combatant is triable for murder and cannot invoke the defense of combatant immunity, it is not clear that the same principle applies in armed conflicts of a non-international nature, where combatant immunity does not apply. The International Criminal Tribunal for the former Yugoslavia (ICTY) has found that war crimes in the context of non-international armed conflict include murder of civilians, but have implied that the killing of a combatant is not a war crime.[57] Similarly, defining as a war crime the "material support for terrorism"[58] does not appear to be supported by historical precedent.

Part IV of the Manual for Military Commissions (M.M.C.) sets forth the elements of crimes defined by the MCA. There are few substantive differences between the M.M.C. definitions and those previously set forth in M.C.I. No. 2. The M.M.C. definition of "Aiding the Enemy" incorporates the element of wrongfulness added by 10 U.S.C. § 950v(26), necessitating a new finding that the accused owed some form of allegiance to the United States at the time the conduct took place. Two crimes, "mutilation or maiming" and "causing serious injury,"[59] were altered to remove the element that required that the victim was in the custody or control of the accused. The new definitions appear to clarify that combat activities, including attacks against combatants, are covered when the accused lacks combatant immunity. The crime "murder by an unprivileged belligerent" was broadened in the definition of "murder in violation of the law of war" to include not just killing, but also deaths resulting from an act or omission of the accused, where the accused intended to kill the victim or victims.

Temporal and Spatial Jurisdiction

The law of war has traditionally applied within the territorial and temporal boundaries of an armed conflict between at least two belligerents.[60] It traditionally has not been applied to conduct occurring on the territory of neutral states or on territory not under the control of a belligerent, to conduct that preceded the outbreak of hostilities, or to conduct during hostilities that do not amount to an armed conflict. Unlike the conflict in Afghanistan, the "Global War on Terrorism" does not have clear boundaries in time or space,[61] nor is it entirely clear who the belligerents are.

The broad reach of the M.O. to encompass conduct and persons customarily subject to ordinary criminal law evoked criticism that the claimed jurisdiction of the military commissions exceeded the customary law of armed conflict, which M.C.I. No. 2 purported to restate.[62] The MCA provides jurisdiction to military commissions over covered offenses "when committed by an alien unlawful enemy combatant before, on, or after September 11, 2001."[63] However, certain definitions used in describing the offenses triable by military commissions would seem to limit many of them to conduct occurring in an armed conflict.

A common element among the crimes enumerated in M.C.I. No.2 was that the conduct "took place in the context of and was associated with armed conflict." The instruction explained that the phrase required a "nexus between the conduct and armed hostilities,"[64] which has traditionally been a necessary element of any war crime. However, the definition of "armed hostilities" was broader than the customary definition of war or "armed conflict." According to the M.C.I., "armed hostilities" need not be a declared war or "ongoing mutual hostilities."[65] Instead, any hostile act or attempted hostile act might have had sufficient nexus if its severity rose to the level of an "armed attack," or if it were intended to contribute to such acts. Some commentators have argued that the expansion of "armed conflict" beyond its customary bounds improperly expanded the jurisdiction of military commissions beyond those that by statute or under the law of war are triable by military commissions.[66] The elements of crimes set forth in the M.M.C. also include a nexus to an armed conflict, but neither the manual nor the MCA contains a definition. The Supreme Court has not clarified the scope of the "Global War on Terrorism," but has not simply deferred to the President's interpretation.

In enacting the MCA, Congress seems to have provided the necessary statutory definitions of criminal offenses to overcome previous objections with respect to subject matter jurisdiction of military commissions. However, questions may still arise with respect to the necessity for conduct to occur in the context of an armed conflict in order to be triable by military commission. There is no express requirement to that effect in the MCA. The overall purpose of the statute together with the elements of some of the crimes arguably may be read to require a nexus.

The definition for "Enemy" provided in M.C.I. No. 2 raised similar issues. According to § 5(B), "Enemy" includes

> any entity with which the United States or allied forces may be engaged in armed conflicts or which is preparing to attack the United States. It is not limited to foreign nations, or foreign military organizations or members thereof. "Enemy" specifically includes any organization of terrorists with international reach.

Some observers argued that this impermissibly subjected suspected international criminals to the jurisdiction of military commissions in circumstances in which the law of armed conflict has not traditionally applied.[67] The distinction between a "war crime," traditionally subject to the jurisdiction of military commissions, and a common crime, traditionally the province of criminal courts, may prove to be a matter of some contention during some of the proceedings.[68] The MCA does not define "enemy." Military commissions trying persons accused of spying or aiding the enemy, for example, face the challenge of determining whether the conduct assisted an "enemy of the United States" as required under the MCA.

COMPOSITION AND POWERS

M.C.O. No. 1 provided for military commissions to consist of panels of three to seven military officers as well as one or more alternate members who had been "determined to be competent to perform the duties involved" by the Secretary of Defense or his designee,[69] and could include reserve personnel on active duty, National Guard personnel in active federal service, and retired personnel recalled to active duty. The rules also permitted the appointment of persons temporarily commissioned by the President to serve as officers in the armed services during a national emergency.[70] The presiding officer was required to be a judge advocate in any of the U.S. armed forces, but not necessarily a military judge.[71]

The MCA provides for a qualified military judge to preside over panels of at least five military officers, except in the cases in which the death penalty is sought, in which case the minimum number of panel members is twelve.[72] Procedures for assigning military judges as well as the particulars regarding the duties they are to perform are left to the Secretary of Defense to prescribe, except that the military judge may not be permitted to consult with members of the panel outside of the presence of the accused and counsel except as prescribed in 10 U.S.C. § 949d. The military judge has the authority to decide matters related to the admissibility of evidence, including the treatment of classified information, but has no authority to compel the government to produce classified information.

Like the previous DOD rules, the MCA empowers military commissions to maintain decorum during proceedings. M.C.O. No. 1 authorized the presiding officer "to act upon any contempt or breach of Commission rules and procedures," including disciplining any individual who violates any "laws, rules, regulations, or other orders" applicable to the commission, as the presiding officer saw fit. Presumably this power was to include not only military and civilian attorneys but also any witnesses who had been summoned under order of the Secretary of Defense pursuant to M.C.O. No. 1 § 5(A)(5).[73] The MCA, 10 U.S.C. § 950w authorizes the military commissions to "punish for contempt any person who uses any menacing word, sign, or gesture in its presence, or who disturbs its proceedings by any riot or disorder." It is unclear whether this section is meant to expand the jurisdiction of military commissions to cover non-enemy combatant witnesses or civilian observers, but the M.M.C. provides for jurisdiction over all persons, including civilians, and permits military judges to sentence those convicted with both fines and terms of confinement.[74] The UCMJ authorizes other military commissions to punish contempt with a fine of $100, confinement for up to 30 days, or both.[75] The M.M.C. does not set a limit on punishment for contempt.

The MCA provides that military commissions have the same power as a general court-martial to compel witnesses to appear in a manner "similar to that which courts of the United States having criminal jurisdiction may lawfully issue."[76] However, rather than providing that the trial counsel and the defense are to have equal opportunity to compel witnesses and obtain evidence, the MCA provides the defense a "reasonable opportunity" to obtain witnesses and evidence. The M.M.C. provides the trial counsel with responsibility for producing witnesses requested by the defense, unless trial counsel determines the witness's testimony is not required, but the defense counsel may appeal the determination to the convening authority or, after referral, the military judge.[77]

Under article 47 of the UCMJ, a duly subpoenaed witness who is not subject to the UCMJ and who refuses to appear before a military commission may be prosecuted in federal court.[78] This article is not expressly made inapplicable to the military commissions established under the MCA. The M.M.C. provides the military judge or any person designated to take evidence authority to issue a subpoena to compel the presence of a witness or the production of documents. As is the case with general courts-martial, the military judge may issue a warrant of attachment to compel the presence of a witness who refuses to comply with a subpoena.[79]

One of the perceived shortcomings of the M.O. had to do with the problem of command influence over commission personnel. M.C.O. No. 1 provided for a "full and fair trial," but contained few specific safeguards to address the issue of impartiality. The President or his designee were empowered to decide which charges to press; to select the members of the panel, the prosecution and the defense counsel, and the members of the review panel; and to approve and implement the final outcome. The President or his designees had the authority to write procedural rules, interpret them, enforce them, and amend them. Justice Kennedy remarked in his concurring opinion that the concentration of authority in the Appointing Authority was a significant departure from the structural safeguards Congress has built into the military justice system.[80]

The MCA, by providing requirements for the procedural rules to guard against command influence, may alleviate these concerns. In particular, the MCA prohibits the unlawful influence of military commissions and provides that neither the military commission members nor military counsel may have adverse actions taken against them in performance reviews. Many of the procedural rules are left to the discretion of the Secretary of Defense or his designee, more so than is the case under the UCMJ. Rule 104 of the Rules for Military Commissions (R.M.C.) prohibits command influence in terms similar to those in the Manual for Courts-Martial, except that they apply more broadly to "all persons" rather than only to "all persons subject to the [UCMJ]."

PROCEDURES ACCORDED THE ACCUSED

M.C.O. No. 1 contained procedural safeguards similar to many of those that apply in general courts-martial, but did not specifically adopt any procedures from the UCMJ, even those that explicitly apply to military commissions.[81] The M.C.O. made clear that its rules alone and *no others* were to govern the trials,[82] perhaps precluding commissions from looking to the UCMJ or other law to fill in any gaps.

Without explicitly recognizing that accused persons had rights under the law, the M.C.O. listed procedures to be accorded to the accused, but specified that these were not to be interpreted to give rise to any enforceable right, benefit or privilege, and were not to be construed as requirements of the U.S. Constitution.[83] Prior to the DTA, the accused had no established opportunity to challenge the interpretation of the rules or seek redress in case of a breach.[84]

The MCA lists a minimum set of rights to be afforded the accused in any trial, and provides the accused an opportunity to appeal adverse verdicts based on "whether the final decision was consistent with the standards and procedures specified" in the MCA, and "to the extent applicable, the Constitution and the laws of the United States." The Department of Defense rules provided the accused was to be informed of the charges sufficiently in advance of trial to prepare a defense;[85] the MCA provides that the accused is to be informed of the charges as soon as practicable after the charges and specifications are referred for trial.[86] The accused continues under the MCA to be presumed innocent until determined to be guilty. As was the case with the previous DOD rules, the presumption of innocence and the right against self-incrimination are to result in an entered plea of "Not Guilty" if the accused refuses to enter a plea or enters a "Guilty" plea that is determined to be involuntary or ill informed.[87] The accused has the right not to testify at trial and to have the opportunity to present evidence and cross-examine witnesses for the prosecution,[88] as was the case under the previous DOD rules.[89]

Open Hearing

The M.C.O. rules provided that the trials themselves were to be conducted openly except to the extent the Appointing Authority or presiding officer closed proceedings to protect classified or classifiable information or information protected by law from unauthorized disclosure, the physical safety of participants, intelligence or law enforcement sources and methods, other national security interests, or "for any other reason necessary for the conduct of a full and fair trial."[90] However, at the discretion of the Appointing Authority, "open proceedings" did not necessarily have to be open to the public and the press.[91]

Because the public, and not just the accused, has a constitutionally protected interest in public trials, the extent to which trials by military commission are open to the press and public may be subject to challenge by media representatives.[92] The First Amendment right of public access extends to trials by court-martial,[93] but is not absolute. Trials may be closed only where the following test is met: the party seeking closure demonstrates an overriding interest that is likely to be prejudiced; the closure is narrowly tailored to protect that interest; the trial court has considered reasonable alternatives to closure; and the trial court makes adequate findings to support the closure.[94]

The MCA provides that the military judge may close portions of a trial only to protect information from disclosure where such disclosure could reasonably be expected to cause damage to the national security, such as information about intelligence or law enforcement sources, methods, or activities; or to ensure the physical safety of individuals.[95] The information to be protected from disclosure does not necessarily have to be classified. To the extent that the exclusion of the press and public is based on the discretion of the military judge without consideration of the constitutional requirements relative to the specific exigencies of the case at trial, the procedures may implicate the First Amendment rights of the press and public. The M.M.C. provides, in Rule 806, that the military judge may close proceedings only to protect information designated for such protection by a government agency or to secure the physical safety of individuals. However, the rule also provides that "in order to maintain the dignity and decorum of the proceedings or for other good cause, the military judge may reasonably limit the number of spectators in, and the means of access to, the courtroom, and exclude specific persons from the courtroom." Such limitations must be supported by written findings.

Although the First Amendment bars government interference with the free press, it does not impose on the government a duty "to accord the press special access to information not shared by members of the public generally."[96] The reporters' right to gather information does not include an absolute right to gain access to areas not open to the public.[97] Access of the press to the proceedings of military commissions may be an issue for the courts ultimately to decide, even if those tried by military commission are determined to lack the protection of the Sixth Amendment right to an open trial or means to challenge the trial.[98]

Right to Be Present

Under UCMJ art. 39,[99] the accused at a court-martial has the right to be present at all proceedings other than the deliberation of the members. Under the DOD rules for military commissions under M.C.O. No. 1, the accused or the accused's civilian attorney could be precluded from attending portions of the trial for security reasons, but a detailed defense counsel was to be present for all hearings. The MCA does not provide for the exclusion of the accused from portions of his trial, and does not allow classified information to be presented to panel members that is not disclosed to the accused. The accused may be excluded from trial proceedings (other than panel deliberations) by the military judge only upon a determination that the accused persists in disruptive or dangerous conduct.[100]

Right to Counsel

As is the case in military courts-martial, an accused before a military commission under both M.C.O. No. 1 and the MCA has the right to have military counsel assigned free of charge. The right to counsel attaches much earlier in the military justice system, where the accused has a right to request an attorney prior to being interrogated about conduct relating to the charges contemplated. Under the MCA, at least one qualifying military defense counsel is to be detailed "as soon as practicable after the swearing of charges…."[101] The accused may also hire a civilian attorney who is a U.S. citizen, is admitted to the bar in any state, district, or possession, has never been disciplined, has a SECRET clearance (or higher, if necessary for a particular case), and agrees to comply with all applicable rules. If civilian counsel is hired, the detailed military counsel serves as associate counsel.[102] Unlike the DOD rules, the MCA provides that the accused has the right to self-representation.[103]

Previous DOD rules provided that defense counsel was to be assigned free of cost once charges were referred, but permitted the accused to request another JAG officer to be assigned as a replacement if available in accordance with any applicable instructions or supplementary regulations that might later be issued.[104] The MCA does not provide the accused an opportunity to request a specific JAG officer to act as counsel. However, the accused may request a replacement counsel from the Chief Defense Counsel if he believes his detailed counsel has been ineffective or if he is otherwise materially dissatisfied with said counsel.[105] If the accused retains the services of a civilian attorney, the MCA provides that military defense counsel is to act as associate counsel.[106] The M.M.C. provides that, in the event the accused elects to represent himself, the detailed counsel shall serve as "standby counsel,"[107] and the military judge may require that such defense counsel remain present during proceedings.[108]

The MCA requires civilian attorneys defending an accused before military commission to meet the same strict qualifications that applied under DOD rules.[109] Under M.C.O. No. 1, a civilian attorney had to be a U.S. citizen with at least a SECRET clearance,[110] with membership in any state or territorial bar and no disciplinary record, and was required to agree in writing to comply with all rules of court.[111] The MCA provides similar requirements,[112] but does not set forth in any detail what rules might be established to govern the conduct of civilian counsel. Under the previous rules, the Appointing Authority and DOD General Counsel were empowered to revoke any attorney's eligibility to appear before any commission.[113] Under the present regulation, the Chief Defense Counsel has the responsibility of determining the eligibility of civilian defense counsel, and may reconsider the determination based on subsequently discovered information indicating material nondisclosure or misrepresentation in the application, or material violation of obligations of the civilian defense counsel, or other good cause."[114] Alternatively, the Chief Defense Counsel may refer the matter to either the convening authority or the DOD Deputy General Counsel (Personnel and Health Policy), who may revoke or suspend the qualification of any member of the civilian defense counsel pool.

The MCA does not address the monitoring of communications between the accused and his attorney, and does not provide for an attorney-client privilege. Rule 502 of the Military Commission Rules of Evidence (Mil. Comm. R. Evid.) provides for substantially the same lawyer-client privilege that applies in courts-martial.[115] With respect to the monitoring of attorney-client communications, the previous DOD rules for military commissions initially provided that civilian counsel were required to agree that communications with the client were subject to monitoring. That requirement was later modified to require prior notification and to permit the attorney to notify the client when monitoring is to occur.[116] Although the government was not permitted to use information against the accused at trial, some argued that the absence of the normal attorney-client privilege could impede communications between them, possibly decreasing the effectiveness of counsel. Civilian attorneys were bound to inform the military counsel upon learning of information about a pending crime that could lead to "death, substantial bodily harm, or a significant impairment of national security."[117] The required agreement under the present regulations imposes a similar duty to inform, but does not mention monitoring of communications.[118]

EVIDENTIARY MATTERS

The Sixth Amendment to the U.S. Constitution guarantees that those accused in criminal prosecutions have the right to be "confronted with the witnesses against [them]" and to have "compulsory process for obtaining witnesses in [their] favor."[119] The Supreme Court has held that "[t]he central concern of the Confrontation Clause is to ensure the reliability of the evidence against a criminal defendant by subjecting it to rigorous testing in the context of an adversary proceeding before the trier of fact."[120] The Military Rules of Evidence (Mil. R. Evid.)[121] provide that "[a]ll relevant evidence is admissible, except as otherwise provided by the Constitution of the United States [and other applicable statutes, regulations and rules]."[122] Relevant evidence is excluded if its probative value is outweighed by other factors.[123] At court-martial, the accused has the right to view any documents in the possession of the prosecution related to the charges, and evidence that reasonably tends to negate the guilt of the accused, reduce the degree of guilt or reduce the punishment,[124] with some allowance for protecting non-relevant classified information.[125]

Supporters of the use of military commissions to try suspected terrorists have viewed the possibility of employing evidentiary standards that vary from those used in federal courts or in military courts-martial as a significant advantage over those courts. The Supreme Court seemed to indicate that the previous DOD rules were inadequate under international law, remarking that "various provisions of Commission Order No. 1 dispense with the principles, articulated in Article 75 [of Protocol I to the Geneva Conventions] and indisputably part of the customary international law, that an accused must, absent disruptive conduct or consent, be present for his trial and must be privy to the evidence against him."[126]

The MCA provides that the "accused shall be permitted to present evidence in his defense, to cross-examine the witnesses who testify against him, and to examine and respond to evidence admitted against him on the issue of guilt or innocence and for sentencing."[127] It is not clear what evidence might be excluded from this requirement as irrelevant to the issues of guilt, innocence, or appropriate punishment. A likely issue will be whether evidence relevant to the credibility of a witness or the authenticity of a document is permitted to be excluded from the accused's right to examine and respond to evidence, unless expressly provided elsewhere in the MCA.

Discovery

The MCA provides that defense counsel is to be afforded a reasonable opportunity to obtain witnesses and other evidence, including evidence in the possession of the United States, as specified in regulations prescribed by the Secretary of Defense.[128] Unlike M.C.O. No. 1, the MCA does not expressly direct the prosecution to provide to the accused all of the evidence trial counsel intends to present.[129] However, as noted above, the accused is entitled to examine and respond to evidence relevant to establishing culpability. Both M.C.O. No. 1 and the MCA provide that the accused is entitled to exculpatory information known to the prosecution, with procedures permitting some variance for security concerns.

Like M.C.O. No. 1, the MCA provides for the protection of national security information during the discovery phase of a trial. The military judge must authorize discovery in accordance with rules prescribed by the Secretary of Defense to redact classified information or to provide an unclassified summary or statement describing the evidence.[130] However, where M.C.O. No. 1 permitted the withholding of any "Protected Information,"[131] the MCA permits the government to withhold only properly classified information that has been determined by the head of a government agency or department to require protection because its disclosure could result in harm to the national security.

Under M.C.O. No. 1, the presiding officer had the authority to permit the deletion of specific items from any information to be made available to the accused or defense counsel, or to direct that unclassified summaries of protected information be prepared.[132] The accused was to have access to protected information to be used by the prosecution and exculpatory protected information "to the extent consistent with national security, law enforcement interests, and applicable law."[133] Defense counsel was permitted to view the classified version only if the evidence was to be admitted at trial. The MCA does not provide defense counsel with access to the classified information that serves as the basis for substitute or redacted proffers.

The MCA provides for the mandatory production of exculpatory information known to trial counsel (defined as exculpatory evidence that the prosecution would be required to disclose in a general court-martial[134]), but does not permit defense counsel or the accused to view classified information. The military judge is authorized to permit substitute information, in particular when trial counsel moves to withhold information pertaining to the sources, methods, or activities by which the information was acquired. If the military judge finds that evidence is classified, he or she must authorize the trial counsel to protect the sources and methods by which such evidence was acquired.[135] The military judge may (but need not) require that the defense and the commission members be permitted to view an unclassified summary of the sources, methods, or activities, to the extent practicable and consistent with national security.[136]

R.M.C. 701(e) provides that trial counsel must provide exculpatory evidence that he would be required to produce in general courts-martial, subject to exceptions where the government asserts a national security privilege. In such a case, the military judge may issue a protective order, but the defense is entitled to an adequate substitute for the information.[137] Such a substitute may involve, to the extent practicable, the deletion of specified items of classified information from documents made available to the defense; the substitution of a portion or summary of the information for such classified documents; or the substitution of a statement admitting relevant facts that the classified information would tend to prove.[138]

In the event the military judge determines that the government's proposed substitute would be inadequate or impracticable for use in lieu of evidence that the government seeks to introduce at trial, evidence that is exculpatory, or evidence that is necessary to enable the defense to prepare for trial, and the government objects to methods the judge deems appropriate, the judge is required to "issue any order that the interests of justice require."[139] Such an order must give the government an opportunity to comply to avoid a sanction, and may include striking or precluding all or part of a witness's testimony, declaring a mistrial, ruling against the government on any issue as to which the evidence is probative and material to the defense, or dismiss charges, or at least those charges or specifications to which the evidence relates, with or without prejudice.[140]

Admissibility of Evidence

The standard for the admissibility of evidence in the MCA remains as it was stated in the M.O.; evidence is admissible if it is deemed to have "probative value to a reasonable person."[141] However, the MCA provides that the military judge is to exclude evidence if its probative value is substantially outweighed by the "danger of unfair prejudice, confusion of the issues, or misleading the commission"; or by "considerations of undue delay, waste of time, or needless presentation of cumulative evidence."[142]

Coerced Statements

M.C.O. No. 1 did not specifically preclude the admission of coerced evidence. In March 2006, DOD released M.C.I. No. 10 prohibiting prosecutors from introducing, and military commissions from admitting, statements established to have been made as a result of torture.

The MCA prohibits the use of statements obtained through torture as evidence in a trial, except as proof of torture against a person accused of committing torture. For information obtained through coercion that does not amount to torture, the MCA provides a different standard for admissibility depending on whether the statement was obtained prior to or after the enactment of the DTA. Statements elicited through such methods prior to the DTA are admissible if the military judge finds the "totality of circumstances under which the statement was made renders it reliable and possessing sufficient probative value" and "the interests of justice would best be served" by admission of the statement. Statements taken after passage of the DTA are admissible if, in addition to the two criteria above, the military judge finds that "the interrogation methods used to obtain the statement do not violate the cruel, unusual, or inhumane treatment or punishment prohibited by the Fifth, Eighth, and Fourteenth Amendments to the U.S. Constitution."

Accordingly, Mil. Comm. R. Evid. 304 provides that an accused's statements that were elicited by torture may not be admitted against him if he makes a timely motion to suppress or an objection to the evidence. Statements introduced by any party that are allegedly produced by lesser forms of coercion, where the degree of coercion is disputed, may only be introduced after the military judge makes the appropriate findings according to the above formula. The defense is required to make any objections to the proposed use of any statements by the accused prior to entering a plea, if the trial counsel has disclosed the intent to use the statement, otherwise the objection will be deemed to have been waived.[143] The military judge may require the defense to establish the grounds for excluding the statement. However, the government has the burden of establishing the admissibility of the evidence. If the statement is ruled admissible, the defense is permitted to present evidence with respect to the voluntariness of the statement, and the military judge must instruct the members to consider that factor in according weight to the evidence. Testimony given by the accused for the purpose of denying having made a statement or for disputing the admissibility of a statement is not to be used against him for any purpose other than in prosecution for perjury or false statements.[144]

Mil. Comm. R. Evid. 304 is modeled on Mil. R. Evid. 304, which prescribes rules for courts-martial to provide for the admission into evidence of confessions and admissions (self-incriminating statements not amounting to an admission of guilt). Under court-martial rules, such a statement and any evidence derived as a result of such a statement are admissible only if the statement was made voluntarily.

convening authority after the introduction of evidence but prior to a finding, through no fault of the accused, or if there is a finding of not guilty, the trial is considered complete for purposes of jeopardy, and the accused may not be tried again for the same charge by any U.S. military or federal court without the consent of the accused.[193] Although M.C.O. No. 1 provided that an authenticated verdict[194] of not guilty by the commission could not be changed to guilty,[195] the rules allowed either the Secretary of Defense or the President to disapprove the finding and return the case for "further proceedings" prior to the findings' becoming final, regardless of the verdict. The possibility that a finding of not guilty could be referred back to the commission for rehearing may have had double jeopardy implications.[196]

Like M.C.O. No. 1, the MCA provides that "[n]o person may, without his consent, be tried by a military commission under this chapter a second time for the same offense."[197] Jeopardy attaches when a guilty finding becomes final after review of the case has been fully completed. The MCA prevents double jeopardy by expressly eliminating the possibility that a finding that amounts to a verdict of not guilty is subject to reversal by the convening authority or to review by the CMCR or the D.C. Circuit. The severity of a sentence adjudged by the military commission cannot be increased on rehearing unless the sentence prescribed for the offense is mandatory.[198] These protections are covered in Chapter XI of the Rules for Military Commission. Proceedings are not authorized to reconsider any ruling that amounts to a finding of not guilty as to any charge or specification, except with respect to a charge where the record indicates guilt as to a specification that may be charged as a separate offense under the MCA.[199] Proceedings for increasing the severity of a sentence are not permitted unless the commission failed to adjudge a proper sentence under the MCA or the sentence was less than that agreed to in a plea agreement.[200]

M.C.O. No. 1 did not provide a specific form for the charges, and did not require that they be authenticated by an oath or signature.[201] The inadequacy of an indictment in specifying charges could raise double jeopardy concerns.[202] If the charge does not adequately describe the offense, another trial for the same offense under a new description is not as easily prevented. The MCA requires that charges and specifications be signed under oath by a person with personal knowledge or reason to believe that matters set forth therein are true.[203] The charges must be served on the accused written in a language he understands.[204] There is no express requirement regarding the specificity of the charges in the MCA, but the Rules for Military Commission provide that the charge must state the punitive article of the act, law of war, or offense as defined in the Manual for Military Commissions that the accused is alleged to have violated.[205] A specification must allege every element of the charged offense expressly or by necessary implication.[206] The Rules for Military Commissions make the trial counsel responsible for causing the accused to be served a copy of the charges in English and another language that the accused understands, where appropriate.[207] After the accused is arraigned, the military judge may permit minor changes in the charges and specifications before findings are announced if no substantial right of the accused is prejudiced, but no major changes may be made over the objection of the accused without a new referral.[208]

The M.O. also left open the possibility that a person subject to the order might be transferred at any time to some other governmental authority for trial.[209] A federal criminal trial, as a trial conducted under the same sovereign as a military commission, could have double jeopardy implications if the accused had already been tried by military commission for the same crime or crimes, even if the commission proceedings did not result in a final verdict. The federal court would face the issue of whether jeopardy had already attached prior to the transfer of the individual from military control to other federal authorities. The MCA does not expressly prohibit trial in another forum.

Conversely, the M.O. provided that the President may determine at any time that an individual is subject to the M.O., at which point any state or federal authorities holding the individual would be required to turn the accused over to military authorities. If the accused were already the subject of a federal criminal trial under charges for the same conduct that resulted in jurisdiction over the accused under the MCA, and if jeopardy had already attached in the federal trial, double jeopardy could be implicated by a new trial before a military commission. The MCA does not explicitly provide for a double jeopardy defense under such circumstances, but the Rules for Military Commissions provide the accused a waivable right to move to dismiss charges on the basis that he has previously been tried by a federal civilian court for the same offense.[210]

Chapter 3

PROPOSED LEGISLATION

A number of bills have been introduced in the 110th Congress to amend the MCA. For additional legislation pertaining to detainees and habeas corpus, see CRS Report RL33180, *Enemy Combatant Detainees: Habeas Corpus Challenges in Federal Court*, by Jennifer K. Elsea and Kenneth R. Thomas.

H.R. 1585, the National Defense Authorization Act for Fiscal Year 2008 (as passed by the House of Representatives on May 17, 2007), would require a report within 60 days after enactment that contains a plan for the transfer of each individual presently detained Guantanamo Bay, Cuba, who is or has ever been classified as an "enemy combatant." It would also require a report identifying detainees who are charged with crimes, those who are eligible for release, and those who are not charged but ineligible for release, supplemented by a list of "actions required to be undertaken, by the Secretary of Defense, possibly the heads of other Federal agencies, and Congress, to ensure that detainees who are subject to an order calling for their release or transfer from the Guantanamo Bay facility have, in fact, been released." Section 1057.

H.R. 2543, the Military Commissions Revision Act of 2007, would redefine "unlawful enemy combatant" to mean "a person who has engaged in, attempted, or conspired to engage in acts of armed hostilities or terrorism against the United States or its co-belligerents, and who is not a lawful enemy combatant." It would permit the admission into evidence of statements obtained by a degree of coercion less than torture in military commission only if the military judge finds that

(1) the totality of the circumstances indicates that the statement possesses probative value to a reasonable person;
(2) the interests of justice would best be served by admitting the statement into evidence; and
(3) the interrogation methods used to obtain the statement do not amount to cruel, inhuman or degrading treatment.

The bill would also repeal 10 U.S.C. § 948d(c) so that CSRT determinations would no longer be dispositive for the purpose of establishing jurisdiction of military commissions, and would restore habeas corpus for persons detained as 'enemy combatants' for more than two years and have not been charged with a crime.

S. 1547 and S. 1548, the National Defense Authorization Act for Fiscal Year 2008 (reported by the Senate Armed Services Committee and the Senate Select Committee on Intelligence on June 5 and June 9, respectively), would make CSRTs mandatory for all detainees and would require the Secretary of Defense to provide procedural rules in some ways similar to those prescribed by the MCA for military commissions. Section 1023. Specifically, detainees would have a right to an attorney for CSRT proceedings, would be entitled to obtain evidence and witnesses under rules consistent with those that apply to military commissions, and the detainee's counsel would have an opportunity to view classified evidence, including evidence to be admitted against the detainee and any potentially exculpatory evidence, consistent with the procedures for the protection of classified information in section 949d(f) of title 10, U.S. Code. The detainee would be entitled to have access to all unclassified evidence and "an unclassified summary of the classified evidence admitted against the detainee that is sufficiently specific to provide the detainee a fair opportunity to respond, with the assistance of counsel, to such evidence." Information obtained through torture would not be admissible into evidence before a CSRT. Information obtained through lesser forms of coercion would be admissible under the same standards as in military commissions, amended as described below.

With respect to military commissions, the bills would define "unlawful enemy combatant" to include any alien who has been a "knowing and active participant in an organization that engaged in hostilities against the United States." They would also prohibit the use of information acquired through coercion not amounting to cruel, inhuman or degrading treatment unless the statement is found to be reliable and probative; its admission would best serve the interests of justice; and either

(1) the tribunal determines that the alleged coercion was incidental to the lawful conduct of military operations at the point of apprehension;
(2) the statement was voluntary; or
(3) the interrogation methods used to obtain the statement do not amount to cruel, inhuman, or degrading treatment prohibited by section 1003 of the Detainee Treatment Act of 2005 (42 U.S.C. § 2000dd).

The rules for the admission of hearsay evidence would be amended to eliminate the reference to the requirements and limitations applicable to the disclosure of classified information." Rather than requiring the party opposing admission to demonstrate that the evidence is unreliable or lacking in probative value, the bills would make the military judge responsible for determining whether "the totality of the

was acquired. If the military judge finds that evidence is classified, he or she must authorize the trial counsel to protect the sources and methods by which such evidence was acquired.[135] The military judge may (but need not) require that the defense and the commission members be permitted to view an unclassified summary of the sources, methods, or activities, to the extent practicable and consistent with national security.[136]

R.M.C. 701(e) provides that trial counsel must provide exculpatory evidence that he would be required to produce in general courts-martial, subject to exceptions where the government asserts a national security privilege. In such a case, the military judge may issue a protective order, but the defense is entitled to an adequate substitute for the information.[137] Such a substitute may involve, to the extent practicable, the deletion of specified items of classified information from documents made available to the defense; the substitution of a portion or summary of the information for such classified documents; or the substitution of a statement admitting relevant facts that the classified information would tend to prove.[138]

In the event the military judge determines that the government's proposed substitute would be inadequate or impracticable for use in lieu of evidence that the government seeks to introduce at trial, evidence that is exculpatory, or evidence that is necessary to enable the defense to prepare for trial, and the government objects to methods the judge deems appropriate, the judge is required to "issue any order that the interests of justice require."[139] Such an order must give the government an opportunity to comply to avoid a sanction, and may include striking or precluding all or part of a witness's testimony, declaring a mistrial, ruling against the government on any issue as to which the evidence is probative and material to the defense, or dismiss charges, or at least those charges or specifications to which the evidence relates, with or without prejudice.[140]

Admissibility of Evidence

The standard for the admissibility of evidence in the MCA remains as it was stated in the M.O.; evidence is admissible if it is deemed to have "probative value to a reasonable person."[141] However, the MCA provides that the military judge is to exclude evidence if its probative value is substantially outweighed by the "danger of unfair prejudice, confusion of the issues, or misleading the commission"; or by "considerations of undue delay, waste of time, or needless presentation of cumulative evidence."[142]

Coerced Statements

M.C.O. No. 1 did not specifically preclude the admission of coerced evidence. In March 2006, DOD released M.C.I. No. 10 prohibiting prosecutors from introducing, and military commissions from admitting, statements established to have been made as a result of torture.

The MCA prohibits the use of statements obtained through torture as evidence in a trial, except as proof of torture against a person accused of committing torture. For information obtained through coercion that does not amount to torture, the MCA provides a different standard for admissibility depending on whether the statement was obtained prior to or after the enactment of the DTA. Statements elicited through such methods prior to the DTA are admissible if the military judge finds the "totality of circumstances under which the statement was made renders it reliable and possessing sufficient probative value" and "the interests of justice would best be served" by admission of the statement. Statements taken after passage of the DTA are admissible if, in addition to the two criteria above, the military judge finds that "the interrogation methods used to obtain the statement do not violate the cruel, unusual, or inhumane treatment or punishment prohibited by the Fifth, Eighth, and Fourteenth Amendments to the U.S. Constitution."

Accordingly, Mil. Comm. R. Evid. 304 provides that an accused's statements that were elicited by torture may not be admitted against him if he makes a timely motion to suppress or an objection to the evidence. Statements introduced by any party that are allegedly produced by lesser forms of coercion, where the degree of coercion is disputed, may only be introduced after the military judge makes the appropriate findings according to the above formula. The defense is required to make any objections to the proposed use of any statements by the accused prior to entering a plea, if the trial counsel has disclosed the intent to use the statement, otherwise the objection will be deemed to have been waived.[143] The military judge may require the defense to establish the grounds for excluding the statement. However, the government has the burden of establishing the admissibility of the evidence. If the statement is ruled admissible, the defense is permitted to present evidence with respect to the voluntariness of the statement, and the military judge must instruct the members to consider that factor in according weight to the evidence. Testimony given by the accused for the purpose of denying having made a statement or for disputing the admissibility of a statement is not to be used against him for any purpose other than in prosecution for perjury or false statements.[144]

Mil. Comm. R. Evid. 304 is modeled on Mil. R. Evid. 304, which prescribes rules for courts-martial to provide for the admission into evidence of confessions and admissions (self-incriminating statements not amounting to an admission of guilt). Under court-martial rules, such a statement and any evidence derived as a result of such a statement are admissible only if the statement was made voluntarily.

Involuntary statements are those elicited through coercion or other means in violation of constitutional due process. To be used as evidence of guilt against the accused, a confession or admission must be corroborated by independent evidence.

Hearsay. Hearsay evidence is an out-of-court statement, whether oral, written, or conveyed through non-verbal conduct, introduced into evidence to prove the truth of the matter asserted. M.C.O. No. 1 did not exclude hearsay evidence. The MCA allows for the admission of hearsay evidence that would not be permitted under the Manual for Courts-Martial[145] only if the proponent of the evidence notifies the adverse party sufficiently in advance of the intention to offer the evidence, as well as the "particulars of the evidence (including [unclassified] information on the general circumstances under which the evidence was obtained)."[146] However, the evidence is inadmissible only if the party opposing its admission "clearly demonstrates that the evidence is unreliable or lacking in probative value." An issue that may arise is whether the rules provide for adequate information regarding the source of evidence for an accused to be in a position to refute the reliability of its content.[147]

The rule regarding hearsay is provided in Mil. Comm. R. Evid. 801 to 807. In contrast to the relatively restrictive rule applied in courts-martial, where hearsay is not admissible except as permitted by a lengthy set of exceptions,[148] the military commission rules provide that hearsay *is* admissible on the same basis as any other form of evidence except as provided by these rules or an act of Congress. The rules do not set forth any prohibitions with respect to hearsay evidence. Mil. Comm. Evid. 803 provides that hearsay may be admitted if it would be admissible at courts-martial. Alternatively, hearsay is admissible if the party proffering it notifies the adverse party thirty days in advance of trial or hearing of its intent to offer such evidence and provides any materials in its possession regarding the time, place, and conditions under which the statement was procured. Absent such notice, the military judge is responsible for determining whether the opposing party has been provided a "fair opportunity under the totality of the circumstances."[149] The opposing party may preclude the introduction of such hearsay evidence by demonstrating by a preponderance of the evidence that such hearsay is unreliable under the totality of the circumstances.[150]

Classified Evidence

At military commissions convened pursuant to the MCA, classified information is to be protected during all stages of proceedings and is privileged from disclosure for national security purposes.[151] Whenever the original classification authority or head of the agency concerned determines that information is properly classified and its release would be detrimental to the national security, the military judge "shall authorize, to the extent practicable," the "deletion of specified items of classified information from documents made available to the accused"; the substitution of a

"portion or summary of the information"; or "the substitution of a statement admitting relevant facts that the classified information would tend to prove." The military judge must consider a claim of privilege and review any supporting materials in camera, and is not permitted to disclose the privileged information to the accused.[152]

With respect to the protection of intelligence sources and methods relevant to specific evidence, the military judge is required to permit trial counsel to introduce otherwise admissible evidence before the military commission without disclosing the "sources, methods, or activities by which the United States acquired the evidence" if the military judge finds that such information is classified and that the evidence is reliable. The military judge may (but need not) require trial counsel to present an unclassified summary of such information to the military commission and the defense, "to the extent practicable and consistent with national security."

The MCA does not explicitly provide an opportunity for the accused to contest the admissibility of substitute evidence proffered under the above procedures. It does not appear to permit the accused or his counsel to examine the evidence or a proffered substitute prior to its presentation to the military commission. If constitutional standards required in the Sixth Amendment are held to apply to military commissions, the MCA may be open to challenge for affording the accused an insufficient opportunity to contest evidence. An issue may arise as to whether, where the military judge is permitted to assess the reliability of evidence based on ex parte communication with the prosecution, adversarial testing of the reliability of evidence before the panel members meets constitutional requirements. If the military judge's determination as to reliability is conclusive, precluding entirely the opportunity of the accused to contest its reliability, the use of such evidence may serve as grounds to challenge the verdict.[153] On the other hand, if evidence resulting from classified intelligence sources and methods contains "'particularized guarantees of trustworthiness' such that adversarial testing would be expected to add little, if anything, to [its] reliability,"[154] it may be admissible and survive challenge.

Classified evidence is privileged under Mil. Comm. R. Evid. 505. Commentary to the rule notes that, because the defense has had no opportunity to evaluate the evidence to formulate any objections, "the military judge's consideration must encompass a broad range of potential objections."[155] During the examination of witnesses at trial, the trial counsel may make an objection to any question or motion that might lead to the disclosure of classified information. The military judge is required to take appropriate action, such as reviewing the matter in camera or granting a delay to allow the trial counsel to confer with the relevant agency officer to determine whether the privilege should be asserted. The judge may order that only parts of documents or other materials be entered into evidence, or permit proof of the contents of such materials without requiring introduction into evidence of the original or a duplicate.[156] In the event the defense reasonably expects to disclose classified information at trial, defense counsel must notify the trial counsel and the judge, and is

precluded from disclosing information known or believed to be classified until the government has had a reasonable opportunity to move for an in camera determination as to protective measures.[157]

SENTENCING

M.C.O. No. 1 required the prosecution to provide in advance to the accused any evidence to be used for sentencing, unless good cause could be shown. The accused was permitted to present evidence and make a statement during sentencing proceedings; however, this right did not appear to mirror the right to make an unsworn statement that military defendants may exercise in regular courts-martial,[158] and apparently the statements were subject to cross-examination. The MCA provides that the accused is entitled to have access to evidence relevant to sentencing, but does not provide that the accused must be given the opportunity to make a statement.

Possible penalties under M.C.O. No. 1 included execution,[159] imprisonment for life or any lesser term, payment of a fine or restitution (which may be enforced by confiscation of property subject to the rights of third parties), or "such other lawful punishment or condition of punishment" determined to be proper. Detention associated with the accused's status as an "enemy combatant" was not to count toward serving any sentence imposed.[160] A sentence agreed to by the accused in plea agreements was binding on the commission, unlike regular courts-martial, in which the agreement is treated as the maximum sentence. Similar to the practice in military courts-martial, the death penalty could only be imposed upon a unanimous vote of the commission.[161] In courts-martial involving any crime punishable by death, however, both the conviction and the death sentence must be by unanimous vote.[162]

The MCA provides that military commissions may adjudge "any punishment not forbidden by [it or the UCMJ], including the penalty of death…."[163] It specifically proscribes punishment "by flogging, or by branding, marking, or tattooing on the body, or any other cruel or unusual punishment, ... or [by the] use of irons, single or double."[164] A vote of two-thirds of the members present is required for sentences of up to 10 years. Longer sentences require the concurrence of three-fourths of the members present. The death penalty must be approved unanimously, both as to guilt and to the sentence, by all members present for the vote.

In cases where the death penalty is sought, a panel of 12 members is required (unless the convening authority certifies that 12 members are not "reasonably available" because of physical conditions or military exigencies, in which case no fewer than nine are required), with all members present for the vote agreeing on the sentence. The death penalty must be expressly authorized for the offense,[165] and the charges referred to the commission must have expressly sought the penalty of death.[166] The death sentence may not be executed until the commission

proceedings have been finally adjudged lawful and all appeals are exhausted,[167] and after the President approves the sentence. 10 U.S.C. § 950i(b)-(c). The President is permitted to "commute, remit, or suspend [a death] sentence, or any part thereof, as he sees fit." 10 U.S.C. § 950i(b). For sentences other than death, the Secretary of the Defense or the convening authority are permitted to adjust the sentence downward. 10 U.S.C. § 950i(d).

Chapter X of the Rules for Military Commissions covers sentencing. "Aggravating factors" that may be presented by the trial counsel include evidence that "any offense of which the accused has been convicted comprises a violation of the law of war."[168] Unlike the rules for courts-martial, there is no express opportunity for the trial counsel to present evidence regarding rehabilitative potential of the accused. However, the rules provide that the accused may make a sworn or unsworn statement to present mitigating or extenuating circumstances or to rebut evidence of aggravation submitted by the trial counsel. In the case of an unsworn statement, which may be written or oral, the accused is not subject to cross-examination by the trial counsel.[169]

The death penalty may only be adjudged if expressly authorized for the offense listed or if it is authorized under the law of war, all twelve members of the commission voted to convict the accused, found that at least one of the listed aggravating factors exists, agreed that such factors outweigh any extenuating or mitigating circumstances, and voted to impose the death penalty. Aggravating factors include that "the accused was convicted of an offense, referred as capital, that is a violation of the law of war," that the offense resulted in the death of or substantially endangered the life of one or more other persons, the offense was committed for the purpose of receiving money or a thing of value, the offense involved torture or certain other mistreatment, the accused was also found guilty of another capital crime, the victim was below the age of fifteen, or that the victim was a protected person.[170] Other aggravating circumstances include specific law-of-war violations, which, except for spying, are not to be applied to offenses of which they are already an element.

Post-Trial Procedure

Criticism leveled at the language of the M.O. included concern that it did not include an opportunity for the accused to appeal a conviction and that it seemingly barred habeas corpus relief.[171] Other concerns were that it appeared to allow the Secretary of Defense (or the President) the discretion to change the verdict from not guilty to guilty, and that it did not adequately protect persons from double jeopardy.[172]

circumstances render the evidence more probative on the point for which it is offered than other evidence which the proponent can procure through reasonable efforts, taking into consideration the unique circumstances of the conduct of military and intelligence operations during hostilities."

H.R. 2710 would restore habeas corpus for detainees. It would eliminate the CSRT review procedure, but retain the DTA provision for appealing military commission decisions, in addition to habeas corpus. H.R. 1416 and S. 185, the Habeas Corpus Restoration Act of 2007, would remove habeas corpus restrictions on detainees and clarify that habeas corpus is available to challenge military commission decisions. H.R. 1416 would also strike the prohibition in section 5 of the MCA on the use of the Geneva Conventions as a source of rights in habeas corpus and other court actions against the United States or its officers and employees. H.R. 2826 would amend 28 U.S.C. § 2241(e) to allow habeas corpus actions and requests for injunctive relief against transfer, except in cases of detainees held in an active war zone where the Armed Forces are implementing the Prisoner of War (POW) regulation, AR 190-8, but would prohibit all other court actions by detainees. However, it would also amend the MCA in such a way as to maintain the current limited appeal of military commission decisions, in addition to habeas corpus. H.R. 267, the Military Commissions Habeas Corpus Restoration Act of 2007, would eliminate restrictions on habeas corpus in 28 U.S.C. § 2241(e), but would eliminate jurisdiction over all other actions, except for DTA challenges of CSRT determinations and military commission decisions.

S. 1876, the National Security with Justice Act of 2007, would redefine "enemy combatant" to mean a person who is not a lawful enemy combatant who has engaged in hostilities against the United States; or has purposefully and materially supported hostilities against the United States (other than hostilities engaged in as a lawful enemy combatant). It would expressly exclude from the definition of "enemy combatant" U.S. citizens and aliens lawfully within the United States who are taken into custody there. Section 201. The bill would eliminate the MCA provision for exclusivity of its appeals provisions, 10 U.S.C. § 950g, and would eliminate the provision in the DTA for appeals of status determinations, but would extend a statutory right of habeas corpus to detainees, giving the D.C. Federal District Court jurisdiction to hear challenges to detention and challenges of final decisions of military commissions. Section 301. Habeas corpus challenges would not be permitted by persons detained in a foreign zone of military operations where the Secretary of Defense certifies that the United States is implementing its detainee regulations, Army Regulation 190-8, or any successor regulation.

S. 576 and its companion bill, H.R. 1415, the Restoring the Constitution Act of 2007, would redefine "unlawful enemy combatant" to mean an individual who is not a lawful combatant who "directly participates in hostilities in a zone of active combat against the United States," or who "planned, authorized, committed, or intentionally aided the terrorist acts on the United States of September 11, 2001,"or harbored such a person. The bills would also expressly limit the definition of "unlawful enemy combatant" for use in designating individuals as eligible for trial by military commission.

The bills would require procedural and evidentiary rules for military commissions to conform to the UCMJ except where expressly provided otherwise, and would limit the Secretary of Defense's authority to make exceptions to commission procedures and rules of evidence to those made necessary by unique circumstances of military or intelligence operations during hostilities.

The bills would repeal the authority for civilian attorneys to act as trial (prosecution) counsel in a commission proceeding, but would permit civilian attorneys to act as defense counsel, with the assistance of detailed defense counsel. An accused who elects to represent himself would be authorized to obtain the assistance of civilian counsel in addition to detailed defense counsel.

The bills would modify the evidentiary requirements of the MCA in several respects. The provision for permitting evidence acquired without a warrant would not apply to evidence acquired within the United States. The responsibility for determining the reliability of hearsay evidence would fall on the military judge, on motion of counsel, rather than requiring the party opposing the evidence to demonstrate its lack of reliability. All statements obtained through coercion would be inadmissible before a military commission, except against a person accused of coercion. The military judge would have the authority to order trial counsel to disclose to defense counsel the sources, methods, or activities by which witnesses or evidence against the accused was obtained, if he determines that that information might reasonably tend to affect the weight given to the out of court statement by the members of the military commission. The prosecution could withdraw the evidence in lieu of compliance with such an order. If the military judge were to determine that substitute information describing evidence of an exculpatory nature insufficiently protected the accused opportunity for a fair trial, the judge could dismiss some or all of the charges or specifications or take such other action as he deemed necessary in the interest of justice.

Habeas corpus would be available to detainees to challenge their detention, but other causes of action would be eliminated. The bills would route appeals of military commissions to the Court of Appeals for the Armed Forces rather than the Court of Military Commissions Review. They would also eliminate the MCA provision excluding Geneva Conventions as a "source of rights," 10 U.S.C. § 948b(g), replacing it with a provision stating that military commission rules that are determined to be inconsistent with the Geneva Conventions are to have no effect. The MCA would expressly state that the President's authority to interpret the Geneva Conventions is subject to congressional oversight and judicial review. The bills would provide for expedited challenges to the MCA in the D.C. district court.

S. 447, the Federal Death Penalty Abolition Act of 2007, would eliminate the death penalty for crimes triable by military commissions in 10 U.S.C. § 950v(b).

The following tables provide a comparison of the military tribunals under the regulations issued by the Department of Defense, standard procedures for general courts-martial under the Manual for Courts-Martial, and military tribunals as authorized by the Military Commissions Act of 2006. Table 1 compares the legal authorities for establishing military tribunals, the jurisdiction over persons and offenses, and the structures of the tribunals. Table 2, which compares procedural safeguards incorporated in the previous DOD regulations (in force prior to the *Hamdan* decision and the enactment of the MCA) and the UCMJ, follows the same order and format used in CRS Report RL31262, *Selected Procedural Safeguards in Federal, Military, and International Courts*, by Jennifer K. Elsea, in order to facilitate comparison of the proposed legislation to safeguards provided in federal court, the international military tribunals that tried World War II crimes at Nuremberg and Tokyo, and contemporary ad hoc tribunals set up by the UN Security Council to try crimes associated with hostilities in the former Yugoslavia and Rwanda.

Table 1. Comparison of Courts-Martial and Military Commission Rules

	General Courts Martial	Military Commission Order No. 1 (M.C.O.)	Military Commissions Act of 2006
Authority	U.S. Constitution, Article I, § 8.	U.S. Constitution, Article II; Presidential Military Order of Nov. 13, 2001 (M.O).	U.S. Constitution, Article I, § 8.
Procedure	Rules are provided by the Uniform Code of Military Justice (UCMJ), chapter 47, title 10, and the Rules for Courts-Martial (R.C.M.) and the Military Rules of Evidence (Mil. R. Evid.), issued by the President pursuant to art. 36, UCMJ. 10 U.S.C. § 836.	Rules are issued by the Secretary of Defense pursuant to the M.O. No other rules apply (presumably excluding the UCMJ). § 1. The President declared it "impracticable" to employ procedures used in federal court, pursuant to 10 U.S.C. § 836.	The Secretary of Defense may prescribe rules of evidence and procedure for military commissions not inconsistent with the MCA. Rules applicable to courts-martial under the UCMJ are to apply except as otherwise specified. 10 U.S.C. § 949a(a). The Secretary of Defense, in consultation with the Attorney General, may make exceptions to UCMJ procedural rules "as may be required by the unique circumstances of the conduct of military and intelligence operations during hostilities or by other practical need." 10 U.S.C.§ 949a(b). The rules must include certain rights as listed in § 949a(b)(2), but need not include those listed in § 949a(b)(3). Pursuant to the above authority, the Secretary of Defense published the Manual for Military Commissions (M.M.C.), including the Rules for Military Commissions (R.M.C.) and the Military Commission Rules of Evidence (Mil. Comm. R. Evid.).

	General Courts Martial	Military Commission Order No. 1 (M.C.O.)	Military Commissions Act of 2006
Jurisdiction over Persons	Members of the armed forces, cadets, midshipmen, reservists while on inactive-duty training, members of the National Guard or Air National Guard when in federal service, prisoners of war in custody of the armed forces, civilian employees accompanying the armed forces in time of declared war or contingency operation, and certain others, including "persons within an area leased by or otherwise reserved or acquired for the use of the United States." 10 U.S.C. § 802. Individuals who are subject to military tribunal jurisdiction under the law of war may also be tried by general court martial. 10 U.S.C. § 818.	Individual subject to M.O., determined by President to be: 1. a non-citizen, and 2. a member of Al Qaeda or person who has engaged in acts related to terrorism against the United States, or who has harbored one or more such individuals and is referred to the commission by the Appointing Authority. § 3(A).	Any "alien unlawful combatant" is subject to trial by military commission. 10 U.S.C. § 948c. An "unlawful enemy combatant" is "a person who has engaged in hostilities or who has purposefully and materially supported hostilities against the United States or its co-belligerents"; or a person determined to be an unlawful enemy combatant by a CSRT or other competent tribunal established under the authority of the President or the Secretary of Defense, which determination is dispositive of status. 10 U.S.C. §§ 948a and 948d(c). "Lawful combatant" is defined in terms of GPW Art. 4. 10 U.S.C. § 948a(2). R.M.C. 201 and 202 provide for jurisdictional requirements of military commissions in accordance with the MCA.

Table 1. Continued

	General Courts Martial	Military Commission Order No. 1 (M.C.O.)	Military Commissions Act of 2006
Jurisdiction over Offenses	Any offenses made punishable by the UCMJ; offenses subject to trial by military tribunal under the law of war. 10 U.S.C. § 818.	Offenses in violation of the laws of war and all other offenses triable by military commission. § 3(B). M.C.I. No. 2 clarifies that terrorism and related crimes are "crimes triable by military commission." These include (but are not limited to): willful killing of protected persons; attacking civilians; attacking civilian objects; attacking protected property; pillaging; denying quarter; taking hostages; employing poison or analogous weapons; using protected persons as shields; using protected property as shields; torture; causing serious injury; mutilation or maiming; use of treachery or perfidy; improper use of flag of truce; improper use of protective emblems; degrading treatment of a dead body; and rape; hijacking or hazarding a vessel or aircraft; terrorism; murder by an unprivileged belligerent; destruction of property by an unprivileged belligerent; aiding the enemy; spying; perjury or false testimony; and obstruction of justice; aiding or abetting; solicitation; command/superior responsibility -	A military commission has jurisdiction to try any offense made punishable by the MCA or the law of war when committed by an alien unlawful enemy combatant before, on, or after September 11, 2001. 10 U.S.C. § 948d(a). Offenses listed in 10 U.S.C. §§ 950q-w and Par IV of the M.M.C. include the following: murder of protected persons; attacking civilians, civilian objects, or protected property; pillaging; denying quarter; taking hostages; employing poison or similar weapons; using protected persons or property as shields; torture, cruel or inhuman treatment; intentionally causing serious bodily injury; mutilating or maiming; murder in violation of the law of war; destruction of property in violation of the law of war; using treachery or perfidy; improperly using a flag of truce or distinctive emblem; intentionally mistreating a dead body; rape; sexual assault or abuse; hijacking or hazarding a vessel or aircraft; terrorism; providing material support for terrorism; wrongfully aiding the enemy; spying, contempt; perjury and obstruction of

	General Courts Martial	Military Commission Order No. 1 (M.C.O.)	Military Commissions Act of 2006
Composition	A military judge and not less than five members, or if requested, except in capital cases, a military judge alone. R.C.M. 501.	From three to seven members, as determined by the Appointing Authority. § 4(A)(2).	A military judge and at least five members, 10 U.S.C. § 948m; R.M.C. 501, unless the death penalty is sought, in which case no fewer than 12 members must be included, 10 U.S.C. § 949m(c). R.M.C. 501 provides that, in death penalty cases where twelve members are not reasonably available because of physical conditions or military exigencies, the convening authority may approve a commission with as few as 9 members.

Source: Congressional Research Service.

Table 2. Comparison of Procedural Safeguards

	General Courts Martial	Military Commission Order No. 1 (M.C.O.)	Military Commissions Act of 2006	Rules for Military Commissions (R.M.C.)
Presumption of Innocence	If the defendant fails to enter a proper plea, a plea of not guilty will be entered. R.C.M. 910(b). Members of court martial must be instructed that the "accused must be presumed to be innocent until the accused's guilt is established by legal and competent evidence beyond a reasonable doubt." R.C.M. 920(e). The accused shall be properly attired in uniform with grade insignia and any decorations to which entitled. Physical restraint shall not be imposed unless prescribed by the military judge. R.C.M. 804.	The accused shall be presumed innocent until proven guilty. § 5(B). Commission members must base their vote for a finding of guilty on evidence admitted at trial. §§ 5(C); 6(F). The Commission must determine the voluntary and informed nature of any plea agreement submitted by the accused and approved by the Appointing Authority before admitting it as stipulation into evidence. § 6(B).	Before a vote is taken on the findings, the military judge must instruct the commission members "that the accused must be presumed to be innocent until his guilt is established by legal and competent evidence beyond reasonable doubt." 10 U.S.C. § 949*l*. If an accused refuses to enter a plea or pleads guilty but provides inconsistent testimony, or if it appears that he lacks proper understanding of the meaning and effect of the guilty plea, the commission must treat the plea as denying guilt. 10 U.S.C. § 949i.	If the defendant fails to enter a proper plea, a plea of not guilty will be entered. R.M.C. 910(b). Members of military commission must be instructed that the "accused must be presumed to be innocent until the accused's guilt is established by legal and competent evidence beyond a reasonable doubt." R.M.C. 920(e). The accused shall be properly attired in the uniform or dress prescribed by the military judge. Physical restraint shall not be imposed during open sessions unless prescribed by the military judge. R.M.C. 804(d).

	General Courts Martial	Military Commission Order No. 1 (M.C.O.)	Military Commissions Act of 2006	Rules for Military Commissions (R.M.C.)
Right to Remain Silent	Coerced confessions or confessions made in custody without statutory equivalent of Miranda warning are not admissible as evidence, unless a narrow "public safety" exception applies. Art. 31, UCMJ, 10 U.S.C. § 831. Once a suspect is in custody or charges have been preferred, the suspect or accused has the right to have counsel present for questioning. Once the right to counsel is invoked, questioning material to the allegations or charges must stop. Mil. R. Evid. 305(d)(1). The prosecutor must notify the defense of any incriminating statements made by the accused that are relevant to the case prior to the arraignment. Motions to suppress such statements must be	Not provided. Neither the M.O. nor M.C.O. requires a warning or bars the use of statements made during military interrogation, or any coerced statement, from military commission proceedings. Art. 31(a), UCMJ (10 U.S.C. § 831) bars persons subject to it from compelling any individual to make a confession, but there does not appear to be a remedy in case of violation. No person subject to the UCMJ may compel any person to give evidence before any military tribunal if the evidence is not material to the issue and may tend to degrade him. 10 U.S.C. § 831.	Article 31, UCMJ, is expressly made inapplicable. 10 U.S.C. § 948b(d). Confessions allegedly elicited through coercion or compulsory self-incrimination that are otherwise admissible are not to be excluded at trial unless they are inadmissible under section 948r. 10 U.S.C. § 949a(b)(2)(C). Section 948r provides that statements elicited through torture may not be entered into evidence except to prove a charge of torture. Statements obtained prior to the enactment of the DTA through coercion that does not amount to torture is admissible if the military judge finds that the "totality of circumstances under which the statement was made renders it reliable and possessing sufficient probative value" and	A statement obtained by use of torture shall not be admitted into evidence against any party or witness, except against a person accused of torture as evidence that the statement was made. R.M.C. 304. When the degree of coercion inherent in the production of a statement offered by either party is disputed, such statement may be admitted, if obtained before December 30, 2005, only if the military judge finds that (A) the totality of the circumstances renders the statement reliable and sufficiently probative; and (B) the interests of justice would be served. Statements obtained on or after December 30, 2005, may be admitted only if the military judge finds that, in addition to (A) and (B) above, (C) the interrogation methods used to

Table 2. Continued

	General Courts Martial	Military Commission Order No. 1 (M.C.O.)	Military Commissions Act of 2006	Rules for Military Commissions (R.M.C.)
	made prior to pleading. Mil. R. Evid. 304. Interrogations conducted by foreign officials do not require warnings or presence of counsel unless the interrogation is instigated or conducted by U.S. military personnel. Mil. R. Evid. 305.		"the interests of justice would best be served" by admission of the statement. Statements taken after passage of the DTA are admissible if the military judge also finds that "the interrogation methods used to obtain the statement do not violate the cruel, unusual, or inhumane treatment or punishment prohibited by the Fifth, Eighth, and Fourteenth Amendments to the U.S. Constitution." 10 U.S.C. § 948r.	obtain the statement do not amount to cruel, inhuman, or degrading treatment. R.M.C. 304(c).
Freedom from Unreasonable Searches & Seizures	"Evidence obtained as a result of an unlawful search or seizure ... is inadmissible against the accused ..." unless certain exceptions apply. Mil. R. Evid. 311. "Authorization to search" may be oral or written, and may be issued by a military judge or an officer in command of the area	Not provided; no exclusionary rule appears to be available. However, monitored conversations between the detainee and defense counsel may not be communicated to persons involved in prosecuting the accused or used at trial. M.C.O. No. 3.	Not provided. Evidence is generally permitted if it has probative value to a reasonable person. 10 U.S.C. § 949a. Procedural rules may provide that evidence gathered without authorization or a search warrant may be admitted into evidence. 10 U.S.C. § 949a.	Not provided. Evidence is probative if "a reasonable person would regard the evidence as making the existence of any fact that is of consequence to a determination of the commission action more probable or less probable than it would be without the evidence." Mil. Comm. R. Evid. 401. Such evidence is

	General Courts Martial	Military Commission Order No. 1 (M.C.O.)	Military Commissions Act of 2006	Rules for Military Commissions (R.M.C.)
	to be searched, or if the area is not under military control, with authority over persons subject to military law or the law of war. It must be based on probable cause. Mil. R. Evid. 315. Interception of wire and oral communications within the United States requires judicial application in accordance with 18 U.S.C. §§ 2516 *et seq.* Mil. R. Evid. 317. A search conducted by foreign officials is unlawful only if the accused is subject to "gross and brutal treatment." Mil. R. Evid. 311(c).	No provisions for determining probable cause or issuance of search warrants are included. Insofar as searches and seizures take place outside of the United States against non-U.S. persons, the Fourth Amendment may not apply. United States v. Verdugo-Urquidez, 494 U.S. 259 (1990).		generally admissible unless its probative value is outweighed by the danger of unfair prejudice, confusion of the issues, or misleading the commission; or by considerations of undue delay, waste of time, or needless presentation of cumulative evidence. Mil. Comm. R. Evid. 402 - 403. There is no prohibition against using evidence gathered without authorization.
Effective Assistance of Counsel	The defendant has a right to military counsel at government expense. The defendant may choose counsel, if that attorney is reasonably available, and	M.C.O. 1 provides that the accused must be represented "at all relevant times" (presumably, once charges are approved until findings are	At least one qualifying military defense counsel is to be detailed "as soon as practicable after the swearing of charges…." 10 U.S.C. § 948k.	Ordinarily, only persons certified under the UCMJ as competent to perform duties in courts-martial may be assigned duties as defense counsel.

Table 2. Continued

	General Courts Martial	Military Commission Order No. 1 (M.C.O.)	Military Commissions Act of 2006	Rules for Military Commissions (R.M.C.)
	may hire a civilian attorney in addition to military counsel. Art 38, UCMJ, 10 U.S.C. § 838. Appointed counsel must be certified as qualified and may not be someone who has taken any part in the investigation or prosecution, unless explicitly requested by the defendant. Art. 27, UCMJ, 10 U.S.C. § 827. In espionage cases or other cases in which classified information may be necessary to prove a charge or defense, the defense is permitted to request the information and to have the military judge review *in camera* information for which the government asserts a privilege. The accused and the defense attorney are entitle to be present for such *in camera*	final — but not for individuals who are detained but not charged) by detailed defense counsel. § 4(C)(4). The accused is assigned a military judge advocate to serve as counsel, but may request to replace or augment the detailed counsel with a specific officer, if that person is available. § 4(C)(3)(a). The accused may also hire a civilian attorney who is a U.S. citizen, is admitted to the bar in any state, district, or possession, has a SECRET clearance (or higher, if necessary for a particular case), and agrees to comply with all applicable rules. The civilian attorney does not replace the detailed counsel,	The accused may also hire a civilian attorney who is 1. a U.S. citizen, 2. admitted to the bar in any state, district, or possession, 3. has never been disciplined, 4. has a SECRET clearance (or higher, if necessary for a particular case), and 5. agrees to comply with all applicable rules. 10 U.S.C. § 949c(b)(3). If civilian counsel is hired, the detailed military counsel serves as associate counsel. 10 U.S.C. § 949c(b)(5). No attorney-client privilege is mentioned. Adverse personnel actions may not be taken against defense attorneys because of the zeal	Civilian counsel must meet MCA qualifications. R.M.C. 502(d). The accused may hire civilian counsel at no expense to the government. R.M.C. 506(a). If civilian counsel is hired, detailed military counsel serves as associate counsel unless excused by the military judge. R.M.C. 502(d)(2). The authority competent to detail defense counsel may excuse or change such counsel, once an attorney client relationship has been formed, only upon the request of the accused or counsel. R.M.C. 505(d)(2).

	General Courts Martial	Military Commission Order No. 1 (M.C.O.)	Military Commissions Act of 2006	Rules for Military Commissions (R.M.C.)
	hearings, and although the government is not generally required to give them access to the classified information itself, the military judge may disapprove of any summary the government provides for the purpose of permitting the defense to prepare adequately for the hearing, and may subject the government to sanctions if it declines to make the necessary information available. Mil. R. Evid. 505.	and is not guaranteed access to classified evidence or closed hearings. § 4(C)(3)(b). Defense Counsel may present evidence at trial and cross-examine witnesses for the prosecution. § 5(I). The Appointing Authority must order such resources be provided to the defense as he deems necessary for a full and fair trial." § 5(H).	with which such officer, in acting as counsel, represented any accused before a military commission…." 10 U.S.C. § 949b. There is a right to self-representation, provided the accused conforms to rules and proper decorum. 10 U.S.C. § 949a.	There is a lawyer-client privilege with respect to confidential matters pertaining to the legal representation unless the communication involves the future commission of a crime or fraud. Mil. Comm. R. Evid. 502. No person may attempt to coerce or, by any unauthorized means, influence the exercise of professional judgment by defense counsel. Defense counsel may not receive unfavorable ratings in performance evaluations due to the zeal with which they represent their clients. R.M.C. 104.

Table 2. Continued

	General Courts Martial	Military Commission Order No. 1 (M.C.O.)	Military Commissions Act of 2006	Rules for Military Commissions (R.M.C.)
	The military judge may order all persons requiring security clearances to cooperate with investigatory personnel in any investigations which are necessary to obtain the security clearance necessary to participate in the proceedings. Mil. R. Evid. 505(g). The attorney-client privilege is honored. Mil. R. Evid. 502.	Communications between defense counsel and the accused are subject to monitoring by the government. Although information obtained through such monitoring may not be used as evidence against the accused, M.C.I. No. 3, the monitoring could arguably have a chilling effect on attorney-client conversations, possibly hampering the ability of defense counsel to provide effective representation.		The accused may elect to conduct the defense personally, but a waiver of the right to counsel must be accepted by the military judge only upon finding that the accused is competent to understand the disadvantages of self-representation and that the waiver is voluntary and understanding. The military judge may require that a defense counsel remain as stand-by counsel. The right of self- representation may be revoked if the accused is disruptive or fails to follow basic rules of decorum and procedure. R.M.C. 506.

	General Courts Martial	Military Commission Order No. 1 (M.C.O.)	Military Commissions Act of 2006	Rules for Military Commissions (R.M.C.)
Right to Indictment and Presentment	The right to indictment by grand jury is explicitly excluded in "cases arising in the land or naval forces." Amendment V. However, a process similar to a grand jury is required by article 32, UCMJ. 10 U.S.C. § 832. Whenever an offense is alleged, the commander is responsible for initiating a preliminary inquiry and deciding how to dispose of the offense. R.C.M. 303-06. The accused must be informed of the charges as soon as practicable. Art. 30, UCMJ, 10 U.S.C. § 830.	Probably not applicable to military commissions, provided the accused is an enemy belligerent. *See Ex parte* Quirin, 317 U.S. 1 (1942). The Office of the Chief Prosecutor prepares charges for referral by the Appointing Authority. § 4(B). There is no requirement for an impartial investigation prior to a referral of charges. The Commission may adjust a charged offense in a manner that does not change the nature or increase the seriousness of the charge. § 6(F).	Article 32, UCMJ, hearings are expressly made inapplicable. 10 U.S.C. § 948b(d)(1)(C). Charges and specifications against an accused are to be signed by a person subject to UCMJ swearing under oath that the signer has "personal knowledge of, or reason to believe, the matters set forth therein," and that they are "true in fact to the best of his knowledge and belief." The accused is to be informed of the charges and specifications against him as soon as practicable after charges are sworn. 10 U.S.C. § 948q.	Upon the swearing of the charges and specifications, the accused is to be informed of the charges against him as soon as practicable in English and, if appropriate, in another language that the accused understands. R.M.C. 308. Charges must be sworn under oath by a person subject to the UCMJ with personal knowledge or reason to believe they are true. R.M.C. 307(b). A specification is "a plain, concise, and definite statement of the essential facts constituting the offense charged. A specification is sufficient if it alleges every element of the charged offense expressly or by necessary implication." R.M.C. 307.

Table 2. Continued

	General Courts Martial	Military Commission Order No. 1 (M.C.O.)	Military Commissions Act of 2006	Rules for Military Commissions (R.M.C.)
Right to Written Statement of Charges	Charges and specifications must be signed under oath and made known to the accused as soon as practicable. Art. 30, UCMJ, 10 U.S.C. § 830.	Copies of approved charges are provided to the accused and Defense Counsel in English and another language the accused understands, if appropriate. § 5(A).	Trial counsel is responsible for serving on counsel a copy of the charges upon the accused, in English and, if appropriate, in another language that the accused understands, "sufficiently in advance of trial to prepare a defense." 10 U.S.C. § 948s.	The trial counsel assigned to a case must cause to be served upon the accused and military defense counsel a copy of the charges, in English and, if appropriate, in another language that the accused understands, sufficiently in advance of trial to prepare a defense. R.M.C. 602.
Right to Be Present at Trial	The presence of the accused is required during arraignment, at the plea, and at every stage of the court-martial unless the accused waives the right by voluntarily absenting him or herself from the proceedings after the arraignment or by persisting in conduct that justifies the trial judge in ordering the removal of the accused from the proceedings. R.C.M. 801. The government may introduce redacted or	The accused may be present at every stage of trial before the Commission unless the Presiding Officer excludes the accused because of disruptive conduct or for security reasons, or "any other reason necessary for the conduct of a full and fair trial." §§ 4(A)(5)(a); 5(K); 6B(3).	The accused has the right to be present at all sessions of the military commission except deliberation or voting, unless exclusion of the accused is permitted under § 949d. 10 U.S.C. § 949a(b)(1)(B). The accused may be excluded from attending portions of the proceeding if the military judge determines that the accused persists in disruptive or dangerous conduct. 10 U.S.C. § 949d(e).	The accused is required to be present at the arraignment, the time of the plea, every stage of the trial including sessions conducted without members (except for certain *in camera* and *ex parte* presentations as may be permitted under R.M.C. 701-703 and Mil. Comm. R. Evid. 505), *voir dire* and challenges of members, the announcement of findings, sentencing proceedings, and post-trial sessions, if any, unless voluntary absence is

	General Courts Martial	Military Commission Order No. 1 (M.C.O.)	Military Commissions Act of 2006	Rules for Military Commissions (R.M.C.)
	summarized versions of evidence to be substituted for classified information properly claimed under privilege, but there is no provision that would allow court-martial members (other than the non-voting military judge) to view evidence that is not seen by the accused. Mil. R. Evid. 505.			permitted by the rules or the accused is excluded by the military judge, after warning, for disruptive conduct. R.M.C. 804.
Prohibition against Ex Post Facto Crimes	Courts-martial will not enforce an ex post facto law, including increasing amount of pay to be forfeited for specific crimes. United States v. Gorki, 47 M.J. 370 (1997).	Not provided, but may be implicit in restrictions on jurisdiction over offenses. *See* § 3(B). M.C.I. No. 2 § 3(A) provides that "no offense is cognizable in a trial by military commission if that offense did not exist prior to the conduct in question."	Crimes punishable by military commissions under the new chapter are contained in subchapter VII. It includes the crime of conspiracy, which a plurality of the Supreme Court in *Hamdan v. Rumsfeld* viewed as invalid as a charge of war crimes. 126 S.Ct. 2749 (2006). The act declares that it "codif[ies] offenses that have traditionally been triable by military commissions," and that "because the [defined crimes]	Crimes and their elements are set forth in Part IV of the M.M.C. Military commissions have jurisdiction to try any offense made punishable by the MCA or the law of war when committed by an alien unlawful enemy combatant before, on, or after September 11, 2001. R.M.C. 201(b)(1).

Table 2. Continued

	General Courts Martial	Military Commission Order No. 1 (M.C.O.)	Military Commissions Act of 2006	Rules for Military Commissions (R.M.C.)
			(including provisions that incorporate definitions in other provisions of law) are declarative of existing law, they do not preclude trial for crimes that occurred before the date of enactment." 10 U.S.C. § 950p. The MCA expressly provides jurisdiction over the defined crimes, whether committed prior to, on or after September 11, 2001. 10 U.S.C. § 948d.	
Protection against Double Jeopardy	Double jeopardy clause applies. See Wade v. Hunter, 336 US 684, 688-89 (1949). Art. 44, UCMJ prohibits double jeopardy, provides for jeopardy to attach after introduction of evidence. 10 U.S.C. § 844. General court-martial proceeding is considered to be a federal trial for double jeopardy purposes. Double jeopardy does not result from charges brought in state or foreign courts,	The accused may not be tried again by any Commission for a charge once a Commission's finding becomes final. (Jeopardy appears to attach when the finding becomes final, at least with respect to subsequent U.S. military commissions.) § 5(P). However, although a finding of Not Guilty by the Commission may not be changed to Guilty, either the	"No person may, without his consent, be tried by a commission a second time for the same offense." Jeopardy attaches when a guilty finding becomes final after review of the case has been fully completed. 10 U.S.C. § 949h. The United States may not appeal a an order or ruling that amounts to a finding of not guilty. 10 U.S.C. § 950d(a)(2). The convening authority may	The accused may move to dismiss charges on the basis that he has previously been tried by military commission or federal civilian court for the same offense. Jeopardy attaches once presentation of evidence on the general issue of guilt has begun, except that a military commission proceeding is not a trial for jeopardy purposes if the military commission lacked

	General Courts Martial	Military Commission Order No. 1 (M.C.O.)	Military Commissions Act of 2006	Rules for Military Commissions (R.M.C.)
	although court- martial in such cases is disfavored. U. S. v. Stokes, 12 M.J. 229 (C.M.A. 1982). Once military authorities have turned service member over to civil authorities for trial, military may have waived jurisdiction for that crime, although it may be possible to charge the individual for another crime arising from the same conduct. *See* 54 AM. JUR. 2D, Military and Civil Defense §§ 227-28.	reviewing panel, the Appointing Authority, the Secretary of Defense, or the President may return the case for "further proceedings" prior to the findings' becoming final. If a finding of Not Guilty is vacated and retried, double jeopardy may be implicated. The order does not specify whether a person already tried by any other court or tribunal may be tried by a military commission under the M.O. The M.O. reserves for the President the authority to direct the Secretary of Defense to transfer an individual subject to the M.O. to another governmental authority, which is not precluded by the order from prosecuting the individual. This subsection could be read to authorize prosecution by federal	not revise findings or order a rehearing in any case to reconsider a finding of not guilty of any specification or a ruling which amounts to a finding of not guilty, or reconsider a finding of not guilty of any charge, unless there has been a finding of guilty under a specification laid under that charge, which sufficiently alleges a violation. The convening authority may not increase the severity of the sentence unless the sentence prescribed for the offense is mandatory. 10 U.S.C. § 950b(d)(2)(B).	jurisdiction, or, if a military commission makes a finding of guilty, the proceeding is not a trial for jeopardy purposes until final review has been fully completed. R.M.C. 907. The convening authority may not order new proceedings to reconsider any ruling that amounts to a finding of not guilty as to any charge or specification, except with respect to a charge where the record indicates guilt as to a specification that may be charged as a separate offense under the MCA. Proceedings for increasing the severity of a sentence are not permitted unless the commission failed to adjudge a proper sentence under the MCA or the sentence was less than that agreed to in a plea agreement. R.M.C. 1102(c).

Table 2. Continued

	General Courts Martial	Military Commission Order No. 1 (M.C.O.)	Military Commissions Act of 2006	Rules for Military Commissions (R.M.C.)
		authorities after the individual was subject to trial by military commission, although a federal court would likely dismiss such a case on double jeopardy grounds. M.O. § 7(e).		
Speedy & Public Trial	In general, accused must be brought to trial within 120 days of the preferral of charges or the imposition of restraint, whichever date is earliest. R.C.M. 707(a). The right to a public trial applies in courts-martial but is not absolute. R.C.M. 806. The military trial judge may exclude the public from portions of a proceeding for the purpose of protecting classified information if the prosecution demonstrates an overriding need to do so and the closure is no broader than necessary. United States v. Grunden, 2 M.J. 116 (CMA 1977); Mil. R. Evid. 505(j).	The Commission is required to proceed expeditiously, "preventing any unnecessary interference or delay." § 6(B)(2). Failure to meet a specified deadline does not create a right to relief. § 10. The rules do not prohibit detention without charge, or require charges to be brought within a specific time period. Proceedings "should be open to the maximum extent possible," but the Appointing Authority has broad discretion to close hearings, and may exclude the public or accredited press from open proceedings. § 6(B)(3).	There is no right to a speedy trial. Article 10, UCMJ, 10 U.S.C. § 810, is expressly made inapplicable to military commissions. 10 U.S.C. § 948b(c). The military judge may close all or part of a trial to the public only after making a determination that such closure is necessary to protect information, the disclosure of which would be harmful to national security interests, or to protect the physical safety of any participant. 10 U.S.C. § 949d(d).	There is a right to a speedy trial, but only after charges are preferred. The accused is to be arraigned within 30 days of the service of charges. The military judge is to set an appropriate schedule for discovery as soon as practicable after the service of charges, and to announce the assembly of the military commission within 120 days of the service of charges. Continuances are to be granted only in the interests of justice, and remedies, such as dismissal of charges (with or without prejudice) may be available. R.M.C. 707. The military judge may close a session to the

	General Courts Martial	Military Commission Order No. 1 (M.C.O.)	Military Commissions Act of 2006	Rules for Military Commissions (R.M.C.)
				public only after specifically finding such closure necessary to protect national security information or to ensure the physical safety of individuals. "Public" includes representatives of the press and representatives of national and international organizations, as determined by the Office of the Secretary of Defense, and certain members of both the military and civilian communities. R.M.C. 806.
Burden & Standard of Proof	Members of court martial must be instructed that the burden of proof to establish guilt is upon the government and that any reasonable doubt must be resolved in favor of the defendant. R.C.M. 920(e).	Commission members may vote for a finding of guilty only if convinced beyond a reasonable doubt, based on evidence admitted at trial, that the accused is guilty. §§ 5(C); 6(F). The burden of proof of guilt is on the prosecution, §5(C); however, M.C.I. No. 2 states that element of	Commission members are to be instructed that the accused is presumed to be innocent until his "guilt is established by legal and competent evidence beyond reasonable doubt"; that any reasonable doubt as to the guilt of the accused must be "resolved in favor of the accused and he must be	Instructions to the members include a charge that the accused must be presumed to be innocent until the accused's guilt is established by legal and competent evidence beyond reasonable doubt; any reasonable doubt must be resolved in favor of the accused, and the burden of

Table 2. Continued

	General Courts Martial	Military Commission Order No. 1 (M.C.O.)	Military Commissions Act of 2006	Rules for Military Commissions (R.M.C.)
		wrongfulness of an offense is to be inferred absent evidence to the contrary. M.C.I. No. 2 § 4(B).	acquitted"; that reasonable doubt as to the degree of guilt must be resolved in favor of the lower degree as to which there is no reasonable doubt; and that the burden of proof is upon the United States. 10 U.S.C. § 949*l*. Two-thirds of the members must concur on a finding of guilty, except in capital cases. 10 U.S.C. § 949m. The military judge is to exclude any evidence the probative value of which is substantially outweighed by the danger of unfair prejudice, confusion of the issues, or misleading the members of the commission, or by considerations of undue delay, waste of time, or needless presentation of cumulative evidence. 10 U.S.C. § 949a.	proof to establish the guilt of the accused is upon the Government. R.M.C. 920(e). A finding of guilty requires the votes of two-thirds of the members present except in capital cases, in which case the vote must be unanimous. R.M.C. 921(c).

	General Courts Martial	Military Commission Order No. 1 (M.C.O.)	Military Commissions Act of 2006	Rules for Military Commissions (R.M.C.)
Privilege against Self-Incrimination	No person subject to the UCMJ may compel any person to answer incriminating questions. Art. 31(a) UCMJ, 10 U.S.C. § 831(a). Defendant may not be compelled to give testimony that is immaterial or potentially degrading. Art. 31(c), UCMJ, 10 U.S.C. § 831(c). No adverse inference is to be drawn from a defendant's refusal to answer any questions or testify at court-martial. Mil. R. Evid. 301(f). Witnesses may not be compelled to give testimony that may be incriminating unless granted immunity for that testimony by a general court-martial convening authority, as authorized by the Attorney General, if required. 18 U.S.C. § 6002; R.C.M. 704.	The accused is not required to testify, and the commission may draw no adverse inference from, a refusal to testify. § 5(F). However, there is no rule against the use of coerced statements as evidence. There is no specific provision for immunity of witnesses to prevent their testimony from being used against them in any subsequent legal proceeding; however, under 18 U.S.C. §§ 6001 *et seq*., a witness required by a military tribunal to give incriminating testimony is immune from prosecution in any criminal case, other than for perjury, giving false statements, or otherwise failing to comply with the order. 18 U.S.C. §§6002; 6004.	"No person shall be required to testify against himself at a commission proceeding." 10 U.S.C. § 948r. Adverse inferences drawn from a failure to testify are not expressly prohibited; however, members are to be instructed that "the accused must be presumed to be innocent until his guilt is established by legal and competent evidence" 10 U.S.C. § 949*l*. There does not appear to be a provision for immunity of witnesses.	No person shall be required to testify against himself at a proceeding of a military commission. R.M.C. 301(a). Testimony can be compelled only if the facts and circumstances are such that no answer the witness might make to the question could incriminate the witness, the witness has waived the privilege, or the privilege against self-incrimination does not apply. A witness may not assert the privilege if the witness is not subject to criminal penalty as a result of an answer by reason of immunity, running of a statute of limitations, or similar reason. Mil. Comm. R. Evid. 301. In the event a witness is granted immunity, the military judge must ensure that the immunity is granted by an

Table 2. Continued

	General Courts Martial	Military Commission Order No. 1 (M.C.O.)	Military Commissions Act of 2006	Rules for Military Commissions (R.M.C.)
				appropriate authority and that the grant provides that neither the testimony of the witness nor any evidence obtained from that testimony may be used against the witness at any subsequent trial other than in a prosecution for perjury, false swearing, the making of a false official statement, or failure to comply with an order to testify after the military judge has ruled that the privilege may not be asserted by reason of immunity. R.M.C. 301.
Right to Examine or Have Examined Adverse Witnesses	Hearsay rules apply as in federal court. Mil. R. Evid. 801 et seq. In capital cases, sworn depositions may not be used in lieu of witness, unless court-martial is treated as non-capital or it is introduced by the defense. Art. 49, UCMJ, 10 U.S.C. § 849. The government may claim a privilege not to	Defense Counsel may cross-examine the prosecution's witnesses who appear before the Commission. § 5(I). However, the Commission may also permit witnesses to testify by telephone or other means not requiring the presence of the witness at trial, in which case cross-	"Defense counsel may cross-examine each witness for the prosecution who testifies before the commission." 10 U.S.C. § 949c. In the case of classified information, the military judge may authorize the government to delete specified portions of evidence to be made available to the accused, or may allow an	The accused has the right to be represented by counsel at oral depositions to examine and cross- examine witnesses. R.M.C. 702(g). "Hearsay may be admitted on the same terms as any other form of evidence ... if it would be admitted under the rules of evidence applicable in trial by general courts-

	General Courts Martial	Military Commission Order No. 1 (M.C.O.)	Military Commissions Act of 2006	Rules for Military Commissions (R.M.C.)
	disclose classified evidence to the accused, and the military judge may authorize the deletion of specified items of classified information, substitute a portion or summary, or statement admitting relevant facts that the evidence would tend to prove, unless the military judge determines that disclosure of classified information itself is necessary to enable the accused to prepare for trial. Mil. R. Evid. 505(g).	examination may be impossible. § 6(D)(2). In the case of closed proceedings or classified evidence, only the detailed defense counsel may be permitted to participate. Hearsay evidence is admissible as long as the Commission determines it would have probative value to a reasonable person. § 6(D)(1). The Commission may consider testimony from prior trials as well as sworn and unsworn written statements, apparently without regard to the availability of the declarant, in apparent contradiction with 10 U.S.C. § 849. § 6(D)(3).	unclassified summary or statement setting forth the facts the evidence would tend to prove, to the extent practicable in accordance with the rules used at general courts- martial. 10 U.S.C. § 949d(f)(2)(A). Hearsay evidence not admissible under the rules of evidence applicable in trial by general courts-martial is admissible only if the proponent notifies the adverse party, sufficiently in advance of its intention to offer the evidence, and the particulars of the evidence (including information on the general circumstances under which the evidence was obtained) unless the party opposing the admission of the evidence "clearly demonstrates that the evidence is unreliable or lacking in probative value." 10 U.S.C. § 949a(b)(2)(E).	martial," or "if the proponent of the evidence makes known to the adverse party" the intention to offer, and the particulars of, the evidence. The accused may have such evidence excluded if he can demonstrate that the evidence is unreliable. Mil. Comm. R. Evid. 802, 803. The military judge may, with respect to classified information, order admission into evidence of only part of a writing, recording or photograph or may order admission into evidence of the whole, writing, recording or photograph with the excision of some or all of the classified information contained therein. Mil. Comm. R. Evid. 505(f)(3). The military judge is required to permit trial counsel to

Table 2. Continued

	General Courts Martial	Military Commission Order No. 1 (M.C.O.)	Military Commissions Act of 2006	Rules for Military Commissions (R.M.C.)
				introduce otherwise admissible evidence before the military commission without disclosing the "sources, methods, or activities by which the United States acquired the evidence" if the military judge finds that such information is classified and that the evidence is reliable. The military judge may (but need not) require trial counsel to present an unclassified summary of such information to the military commission and the defense, "to the extent practicable and consistent with national security." Mil. Comm. R. Evid. 505(e)(6).
Right to Compulsory Process to Obtain Witnesses	Defendants before court-martial have the right to compel appearance of witnesses necessary to their defense. R.C.M. 703. Process to compel witnesses in court-martial cases	The accused may obtain witnesses and documents "to the extent necessary and reasonably available as determined by the Presiding Officer." § 5(H). The	Defense counsel is to be afforded a reasonable opportunity to obtain witnesses and other evidence, including evidence in the possession of the United States, according to	Subject to 10 U.S.C. § 949j(c) and R.M.C. 701, each party is entitled to the production of evidence which is relevant, necessary and noncumulative. R.M.C. 703(f) The defense is

	General Courts Martial	Military Commission Order No. 1 (M.C.O.)	Military Commissions Act of 2006	Rules for Military Commissions (R.M.C.)
	is to be similar to the process used in federal courts. Art. 46, UCMJ, 10 U.S.C. § 846.	Commission has the power to summon witnesses as requested by the defense. § 6(A)(5). The power to issue subpoenas is exercised by the Chief	DOD regulations. The military commission is authorized to compel witnesses under U.S. jurisdiction to appear. The military judge may authorize discovery in accordance with rules prescribed by the Secretary of Defense to redact classified	to have a "reasonable opportunity to obtain witnesses" who have not been deemed "unavailable" by the military judge according to Mil. Comm. R. Evid. 804(a).
		Prosecutor; the Chief Defense Counsel has no such authority. M.C.I. Nos. 3-4.	information or to provide an unclassified summary or statement describing the evidence. The trial counsel is obligated to disclose exculpatory evidence of which he is aware to the defense, but such information, if classified, is available to the accused only in a redacted or summary form, and only if making the information available is possible without compromising intelligence sources, methods, or activities, or other national security interests. 10 U.S.C. § 949j.	Evidence under the control of the Government may be obtained by requesting it from the custodian. Other evidence may be obtained by subpoena. R.M.C. 703. The defense may submit a written request listing witnesses for production by the Government The judge is authorized to grant the production of the witnesses as justice may require. R.M.C. 703(c).

Table 2. Continued

	General Courts Martial	Military Commission Order No. 1 (M.C.O.)	Military Commissions Act of 2006	Rules for Military Commissions (R.M.C.)
Right to Trial by Impartial Judge	A qualified military judge is detailed to preside over the court- martial. The convening authority may not prepare or review any report concerning the performance or effectiveness of the military judge. Art. 26, UCMJ, 10 U.S.C. § 826. Article 37, UCMJ, prohibits unlawful influence of courts- martial through admonishment, censure, or reprimand of its members by the convening authority or commanding officer, or any unlawful attempt by a person subject to the UCMJ to coerce or influence the action of a court-martial or convening authority. Art. 37, UCMJ, 10 U.S.C. § 837.	The Presiding Officer is appointed directly by the Appointing Authority, which decides all interlocutory issues. There do not appear to be any special procedural safeguards to ensure impartiality, but challenges for cause have been permitted. § 4(A)(4). The presiding judge, who decides issues of admissibility of evidence, does not vote as part of the commission on the finding of guilt or innocence. Article 37, UCMJ, provides that no person subject to the UCMJ "may attempt to coerce or, by any unauthorized means, influence the action of a court-martial *or any other military tribunal* or any member thereof, in reaching the findings or sentence in any	Military judges must take an oath to perform their duties faithfully. 10 U.S.C. § 949g. The convening authority is prohibited from preparing or reviewing any report concerning the effectiveness, fitness, or efficiency of a military judge. 10 U.S.C. § 948j(a). A military judge may not be assigned to a case in which he is the accuser, an investigator, a witness, or a counsel. 10 U.S.C. § 948j(c). The military judge may not consult with the members of the commission except in the presence of the accused, trial counsel, and defense counsel, nor may he vote with the members of the commission. 10 U.S.C. § 948j(d). Convening authority may not censure,	Military judges must take an oath to "faithfully and impartially" perform their duties. R.M.C. 807(b). A military judge may not be assigned to a case "if he is the accuser or a witness or has acted as investigator or a counsel in the same case." R.M.C. 502(c)(1). Recusal is required in any proceeding in which a military judge's impartiality might reasonably be questioned. R.M.C. 902(a). "A military judge ... may not consult with the members of the commission except in the presence of the accused, trial counsel, and defense counsel, nor may he vote with the members of the commission." R.M.C. 502(c)(2). The convening authority is

	General Courts Martial	Military Commission Order No. 1 (M.C.O.)	Military Commissions Act of 2006	Rules for Military Commissions (R.M.C.)
		case, or the action of any convening, approving, or reviewing authority with respect to his judicial acts." 10 U.S.C. § 837. M.C.I. No. 9 clarifies that Art. 37 applies with respect to members of the review panel. M.C.I. No. 9 § 4(F).	reprimand, or admonish the military judge. No person may attempt to coerce or use unauthorized means to influence the action of a commission. 10 U.S.C. § 949b. The military judge may be challenged for cause. 10 U.S.C. § 949f.	prohibited from preparing or reviewing "any report concerning the effectiveness, fitness, or efficiency of a military judge ... which relates to his performance of duty as a military judge on the military commission." R.M.C. 502(c)(4). The convening authority may not censure, reprimand, or admonish the military judge. R.M.C. 104(a)(1). "No person may attempt to coerce or, by any unauthorized means, influence the action of a military commission " R.M.C. 104(a)(2).
Right to Trial by Impartial Jury	A military accused has no Sixth Amendment right to a trial by petit jury. *Ex Parte* Quirin, 317 U.S. 1, 39- 40 (1942) (*dicta*). However, "Congress has provided for trial by members at a court- martial." United States v. Witham, 47 MJ 297,	The commission members are appointed directly by the Appointing Authority. While the Commission is bound to proceed impartially, there do not appear to be any special procedural safeguards designed to ensure their impartiality.	Military commission members must take an oath to perform their duties faithfully. 10 U.S.C. § 949g. The accused may make one peremptory challenge, and may challenge other members for cause. 10 U.S.C. § 949f. No convening authority may	Military commission members must take an oath to "faithfully and impartially" perform their duties. R.M.C. 807(b). "Members should avoid any conduct or communication with the military judge, witnesses, or other trial

Table 2. Continued

	General Courts Martial	Military Commission Order No. 1 (M.C.O.)	Military Commissions Act of 2006	Rules for Military Commissions (R.M.C.)
	301 (1997); Art. 25, UCMJ, 10 U.S.C. § 825. The Sixth Amendment requirement that the jury be impartial applies to court-martial members and covers not only the selection of individual jurors, but also their conduct during the trial proceedings and the subsequent deliberations. United States v. Lambert, 55 M.J. 293 (2001). The absence of a right to trial by jury precludes criminal trial of civilians by court-martial. Reid v. Covert, 354 U.S. 1 (1957); Kinsella v. United States *ex rel*. Singleton, 361 U.S. 234 (1960).	However, defendants have successfully challenged members for cause. § 6(B).	censure, reprimand, or admonish the commission or any member with respect to the findings or sentence or the exercise of any other functions in the conduct of the proceedings. No person may attempt to coerce or, by any unauthorized means, influence the action of a commission or any member thereof, in reaching the findings or sentence in any case. Military commission duties may not be considered in the preparation of an effectiveness report or any similar document with potential impact on career- advancement. 10 U.S.C. § 949b.	personnel during the trial which might present an appearance of partiality. Except as provided in [the R.M.C.], members should not discuss any part of a case with anyone until the matter is submitted to them for determination. Members should not on their own visit or conduct a view of the scene of the crime and should not investigate or gather evidence of the offense. Members should not form an opinion of any matter in connection with the case until that matter has been submitted to them for determination." R.M.C. 502(a). The accused may challenge one member peremptorily, and may challenge other members for cause. R.M.C. 912(g).

	General Courts Martial	Military Commission Order No. 1 (M.C.O.)	Military Commissions Act of 2006	Rules for Military Commissions (R.M.C.)
				Convening authority may not censure, reprimand, or admonish the military commission, or any member with respect to the findings or sentence or any other exercise of its or his function in the conduct or the proceedings. R.M.C. 104(a)(1). "No person may attempt to coerce or, by any unauthorized means, influence the action of a military commission " R.M.C. 104(a)(2).
Right to Appeal to Independent Reviewing Authority	Those convicted by court-martial have an automatic appeal to their respective service courts of appeal, depending on the severity of the punishment. Art. 66, UCMJ; 10 U.S.C. § 866. Decisions by service appellate courts are reviewable on a discretionary basis by the Court of Appeals	A review panel appointed by the Secretary of Defense reviews the record of the trial in a closed conference, disregarding any procedural variances that would not materially affect the outcome of the trial, and recommends its disposition to the Secretary of Defense. Although the	The accused may submit matters for consideration by the convening authority with respect to the authenticated findings or sentence of the military commission. The convening authority must review timely submissions prior to taking action. 10 U.S.C. §950b. The accused may appeal	Prior to taking action, the convening authority must consider timely written submissions by the accused concerning "(1) Allegations of errors affecting the legality of the findings or sentence; (2) Portions or summaries of the record and copies of documentary evidence offered

Table 2. Continued

	General Courts Martial	Military Commission Order No. 1 (M.C.O.)	Military Commissions Act of 2006	Rules for Military Commissions (R.M.C.)
	for the Armed Forces (CAAF), a civilian court composed of five civilian judges appointed by the President. Art. 67, UCMJ; 10 U.S.C. § 867. CAAF decisions are subject to Supreme Court review by writ of certiorari. 28 U.S.C. § 1259. The writ of *habeas corpus* provides the primary means by which those sentenced by military court, having exhausted military appeals, can challenge a conviction or sentence in a civilian court. The scope of matters that a court will address is narrower than in challenges of federal or state convictions. Burns v. Wilson, 346 U.S. 137 (1953).	Defense Counsel has the duty of representing the interests of the accused during any review process, the review panel need not consider written submissions from the defense, nor does there appear to be an opportunity to rebut the submissions of the prosecution. If the majority of the review panel forms a "definite and firm conviction that a material error of law occurred," it may return the case to the Appointing Authority for further proceedings. § 6(H)(4). The review panel recommendation does not appear to be binding. The Secretary of Defense may serve as Appointing Authority and as the final reviewing authority, as designated by the	a final decision of the military commission with respect to issues of law to the Court of Military Commission Review, a new body comprised of appellate military judges who meet the same qualifications as military judges orcomparable qualifications for civilian judges. 10 U.S.C. § 950f. Once these appeals are exhausted, the accused may appeal the final decision to the United States Court of Appeals for the District of Columbia Circuit. Appellate court decisions may be reviewed by the Supreme Court under writ of certiorari. 10 U.S.C. § 950g.	or introduced at trial; (3) Matters in mitigation which were not available for consideration at the military commission; and (4) Clemency recommendations by any member, the military judge, or any other person." R.M.C. 1105 After any military commission in which the approved sentence includes death, the accused may not waive or withdraw appellate review. R.M.C. 1110. In cases where appellate review has not been waived, the findings and sentence shall be reviewed by the Court of Military Commission Review for errors of law. Relief may be granted if the "error of law prejudiced a substantial trial

	General Courts Martial	Military Commission Order No. 1 (M.C.O.)	Military Commissions Act of 2006	Rules for Military Commissions (R.M.C.)
		President. Although the M.O specifies that the individual is not privileged to seek any remedy in any U.S. court or state court, the court of any foreign nation, or any international tribunal, M.O. § 7(b), Congress established jurisdiction in the Court of Appeals for the D.C. Circuit to hear challenges to final decisions of military commissions. Detainee Treatment Act of 2005.		right of the accused." R.M.C. 1201(d). The accused may, within twenty days after notification of the decision of the Court of Military Commission Review, petition the United States Court of Appeals for the District of Columbia for a review of the case. R.M.C. 1205(a). Decisions of the D.C. Circuit may be reviewed by the Supreme Court by writ of certiorari. R.M.C. 1205(b).
Protection against Excessive Penalties	The right to appeal a conviction resulting in a death sentence may not be waived. R.C.M. 1110. Death may only be adjudged for certain crimes where the defendant is found guilty by unanimous vote of court-martial members present at the time of the vote. Prior to arraignment, the trial counsel	The accused is permitted to make a statement during sentencing procedures. § 5(M). The death sentence may be imposed only on the unanimous vote of a seven-member panel. § 6(F). The commission may only impose a sentence that is appropriate to the offense for which there	Military commissions may adjudge "any punishment not forbidden by [the MCA] or the law of war, including the penalty of death…." 10 U.S.C. § 948d. A vote two-thirds of the members present is required for sentences of up to 10 years. Longer sentences require the concurrence of three-fourths of	Subject to national security privilege, "the trial counsel shall, as soon as practicable, disclose to the defense the existence of evidence known to the trial counsel which reasonably tends to ... reduce the punishment." R.M.C. 701(e). The right to appeal a conviction resulting in a death

Table 2. Continued

	General Courts Martial	Military Commission Order No. 1 (M.C.O.)	Military Commissions Act of 2006	Rules for Military Commissions (R.M.C.)
	must give the defense written notice of aggravating factors the prosecution intends to prove. R.C.M. 1004. A conviction of spying during time of war under article 106, UCMJ, carries a mandatory death penalty. 10 U.S.C. § 906.	was a finding of guilty, including death, imprisonment, fine or restitution, or "other such lawful punishment or condition of punishment as the commission shall determine to be proper." § 6(G). If the Secretary of Defense has the authority to conduct the final review of a conviction and sentence, he may mitigate, commute, defer, or suspend, but not increase, the sentence. However, he may disapprove the findings and return them for further action by the military commission. § 6(H).	the members present. The death penalty must be approved unanimously on a unanimous guilty verdict. Where the death penalty is sought, a panel of 12 members is required (unless not "reasonably available"). The death penalty must be expressly authorized for the offense, and the charges must have expressly sought the penalty of death. 10 U.S.C. § 949m. An accused who is sentenced to death may not waive or withdraw his appeal to the Court of Military Commission Review. 10 U.S.C. § 950c. The death sentence may not be executed until the commission proceedings have been finally adjudged lawful and the time for filing a writ has expired or the writ has been denied; and the President approves the sentence. 10 U.S.C. § 950i.	sentence may not be waived nor withdrawn. R.M.C. 1110. The convening authority may, if the accused is found guilty, reduce the charge to a lesser included offense, order a rehearing, or set aside the finding of guilt and dismiss the charge. R.M.C. 1107(c). A sentence of up to ten years requires a two-thirds vote of members present. A sentence of more than ten years requires a three-fourths vote. A sentence which includes death requires a unanimous vote. R.M.C. 1006(d)(4). Death sentences may not be executed until approved by the President. R.M.C. 1207(a).

REFERENCES

[1] Rasul v. Bush, 542 U.S. 466 (2004). For a summary of Rasul and related cases, see CRS Report RS21884, The Supreme Court and Detainees in the War on Terrorism: Summary and Analysis of Recent Decisions, and CRS Report RS22466, Hamdan v. Rumsfeld: Military Commissions in the "Global War on Terrorism," both by Jennifer K. Elsea.

[2] Detention, Treatment, and Trial of Certain Non-Citizens in the War Against Terrorism §1(a), 66 Fed. Reg. 57,833 (November 16, 2001) (hereinafter "M.O.").

[3] P.L. 109-148, §1005(e)(1).

[4] Hamdan v. Rumsfeld, 126 S.Ct. 2749 (2006), rev'g 415 F.3d 33 (D.C. Cir. 2005).

[5] 10 U.S.C. § 801 et seq.

[6] P.L. 109-366, 120 Stat. 2600, codified at chapter 47a of title 10, U.S. Code.

[7] Department of Defense, The Manual for Military Commissions, January 18, 2007, available at [http://www.defenselink.mil/pubs/pdfs/ The%20Manual% 20for%20Military% 20Commissions.pdf].

[8] United States v. Khadr, CMCR 07-001 (September 24, 2007), available online at [http://www.defenselink.mil/news/Sep2007/KHADR%20Decision%20(24% 20Sep%200 7)(25%20pages).pdf](last visited September 26, 2007). See infra note 46 and accompanying text.

[9] See CRS Report RL31191, Terrorism and the Law of War: Trying Terrorists as War Criminals before Military Commissions, by Jennifer K. Elsea (providing a general background of U.S. history of military commissions).

[10] See U.S. Army Field Manual (FM) 27-10, The Law of Land Warfare, section 505(e) [hereinafter "FM 27-10"].

[11] See William Winthrop, *Military Law and Precedents* 841-42 (2d ed. 1920)(noting that "in the absence of any statute or regulation," the same principles and

procedures commonly govern, though possibly more "liberally construed and applied"); David Glazier, Note, Kangaroo Court or Competent Tribunal?: Judging the 21st Century Military Commission, 89 VA. L. REV. 2005 (2003).

[12] 10 U.S.C. § 821. There are only two statutory offenses under the Uniform Code of Military Justice (UCMJ) for which convening a military commission is explicitly recognized: aiding the enemy and spying (in time of war). 10 U.S.C. §§ 904 and 906, respectively. The circumstances under which civilians accused of aiding the enemy may be tried by military tribunal have not been decided, but a court interpreting the article may limit its application to conduct committed in territory under martial law or military government, within a zone of military operations or area of invasion, or within areas subject to military jurisdiction. See FM 27-10, supra note 10, at para. 79(b)(noting that treason and espionage laws are available for incidents occurring outside of these areas, but are triable in civil courts). Spying is not technically a violation of the law of war, however, but violates domestic law and traditionally may be tried by military commission. See id. at para. 77 (explaining that spies are not punished as "violators of the law of war, but to render that method of obtaining information as dangerous, difficult, and ineffective as possible").

[13] In re Yamashita, 327 U.S. 1, 17 (1946) ("Obviously charges of violations of the law of war triable before a military tribunal need not be stated with the precision of a common law indictment.").

[14] Reprinted at 41 I.L.M. 725 (2002). A revision was issued August 31, 2005. The Department of Defense (DOD) subsequently released ten "Military Commission Instructions" ("M.C.I. No. 1-10") to elaborate on the set of procedural rules to govern military tribunals. The instructions set forth the elements of some crimes to be tried by military commission, established guidelines for civilian attorneys, and provided other administrative guidance and procedures for military commissions.

[15] See Letter from Timothy H. Edgar, ACLU Legislative Counsel, Military Commission Order No. 1, March 21, 2002 (April 16, 2002), available at [http://www.aclu.org/NationalSecurity/NationalSecurity.cfm?ID=10150&c=111] (last visited August 13, 2007); American College of Trial Lawyers, Report on Military Commissions for the Trial of Terrorists, March 2003 [hereinafter "ACTL"], available at [http://www.actl.com/AM/Template.cfm?Section=All_Publications&Template=/CM/ContentDisplay.cfm&ContentFileID=63] (last visited August 13, 2007); ACTL, Supplemental Report on Military Commissions for the Trial of Terrorists, October 2005, online at [http://www.actl.com/AM/Template.cfm?Section=Home&template=/CM/ContentDisplay.cfm&ContentID=2152] (last visited August 13, 2007).

[16] The Administration has not explicitly used this authority; instead, it characterizes the prisoners as "enemy combatants" detained pursuant to the law of war. See, e.g., Response of the United States to Request for Precautionary Measures - Detainees in Guantanamo Bay, Cuba to the Inter-American Commission on Human Rights, Organization of American States 25 (2002)("It is humanitarian law, and not human rights law, that governs the capture and detention of enemy combatants in an armed conflict.")

[17] See Bruce Zagaris, U.S. Defense Department Issues Order on Military Commissions, 18 No. 5 *Int'l Enforcement L. Rep* 215 (2002) (citing comments by DOD chief counsel William J. Haynes II to a New York Times reporter).

[18] See Neil A. Lewis, Two Prosecutors Faulted Trials For Detainees, NY TIMES, August 1, 2005, at A1.

[19] See Press Release, Department of Defense, President Determines Enemy Combatants Subject to His Military Order (July 3, 2003), available at [http://www.defenselink.mil/ releases/2003/nr20030703-0173.html] (last visited August 13, 2007). According to the Defense Department, that determination is effectively "a grant of [military] jurisdiction over the person." See John Mintz, 6 Could Be Facing Military Tribunals, *Wash. Post*, July 4, 2003, at A1. In 2004, nine additional detainees were determined to be eligible. See Press Release, Department of Defense, Presidential Military Order Applied to Nine more Combatants (July 7, 2004), available at [http://www.defenselink. mil/releases/2004/nr20040707-0987.html] (last visited August 13, 2007). In November 2005, five more detainees were charged. See Press Release, Department of Defense, Military Commission Charges Approved (November 7, 2005), available at [http://www.defenselink.mil/releases/2005/nr20051107-5078.html] (last visited August 13, 2007).

[20] 344 F. Supp.2d 152 (D. D.C. 2004), rev'd 415 F.3d 33 (D.C. Cir. 2005), rev'd 126 S.Ct. 2749 (2006). For a more thorough discussion of the Hamdan case, see CRS Report RS22466, Hamdan v. Rumsfeld: Military Commissions in the 'Global War on Terrorism,' by Jennifer K. Elsea.

[21] 10 U.S.C. §§ 801 et seq.

[22] There are four Conventions, the most relevant of which is The Geneva Convention Relative to the Treatment of Prisoners of War, August 12, 1949, 6 U.S.T. 3317 (hereinafter "GPW").

[23] Rumsfeld v. Hamdan, 415 F.3d 33, 39-40 (D.C. Cir. July 15, 2005).

[24] Authorization for Use of Military Force ("the AUMF"), P.L. 107-40, 115 Stat. 224 (2001).

[25] Hamdan, 415 F.3d at 37.

[26] P.L. 109-148, §1005(e)(1) provides that "no court ... shall have jurisdiction to hear or consider ... an application for ... habeas corpus filed by ... an alien detained ... at Guantanamo Bay." The provision was not yet law when the

appellate court decided against the petitioner, Hamdan v. Rumsfeld, 415 F.3d 33 (D.C. Cir. 2005), rev'd 126 S.Ct. 2749 (2006). At issue was whether this provision applies to pending cases. The Court found that the provision does not apply to Hamdan's petition, but did not resolve whether it affects other cases that fall under the DTA's provisions regarding final review of Combatant Status Review Tribunals. Slip op. at 19, and n.14. For an overview of issues related to the jurisdiction over habeas corpus, see CRS Report RL33180, Enemy Combatant Detainees: Habeas Corpus Challenges in Federal Court, by Jennifer K. Elsea and Kenneth Thomas.

[27] Hamdan, 126 S.Ct. at 2769. To resolve the question, the majority employed canons of statutory interpretation supplemented by legislative history, avoiding the question of whether the withdrawal of the Court's jurisdiction would constitute a suspension of the Writ of Habeas Corpus, or whether it would amount to impermissible "court-stripping." Justice Scalia, joined by Justices Alito and Thomas in his dissent, interpreted the DTA as a revocation of jurisdiction.

[28] 10 U.S.C. § 821 ("The provisions of [the UCMJ] conferring jurisdiction upon courts-martial do not deprive military commissions, provost courts, or other military tribunals of concurrent jurisdiction with respect to offenders or offenses that by statute or by the law of war may be tried by military commissions, provost courts, or other military tribunals."). The Hamdan majority concluded that "compliance with the law of war is the condition upon which the authority set forth in Article 21 is granted." Hamdan, at 2794.

[29] The Court disagreed that the Eisentrager case requires another result, noting that the Court there had decided the treaty question on the merits based on its interpretation of the Geneva Convention of 1929 and that the 1949 Conventions were drafted to reject that interpretation. Hamdan, at 2802-03.

[30] GPW art. 3 § 1(d). The identical provision is included in each of the four Geneva Conventions and applies to any "conflict not of an international character." The majority declined to accept the President's interpretation of Common Article 3 as inapplicable to the conflict with al Qaeda and interpreted the phrase "in contradistinction to a conflict between nations," which the Geneva Conventions designate a "conflict of international character." Hamdan, at 2794-96.

[31] Id. at 2796-97 (plurality opinion); Id. (Kennedy, J., concurring) at 2803. Justice Stevens, joined by Justices Ginsburg, Breyer, and Souter, further based their conclusion on the basis that M.C.O. No. 1 did not meet all criteria of art. 75 of Protocol I to the Geneva Conventions of 1949, adopted in 1977 (Protocol I). While the United States is not party to Protocol I, the plurality noted that many authorities regard it as customary international law.

[32] MCA § 4 (adding to 10 U.S.C. § 836(a) the words "except as provided in chapter 47A of this title" and to § 836(b) the words" except insofar as applicable to military commissions established under chapter 47A of this title").

[33] 10 U.S.C. § 948a (as added by the MCA).

[34] MCA § 4 (amending 10 U.S.C. §§ 821(jurisdiction of general courts-martial not exclusive), 828 (detail or employment of reporters and interpreters), 848 (power to punish contempt), 850(a) (admissibility of records of courts of inquiry), 904(aiding the enemy), and 906(spying)).

[35] 10 U.S.C. § 948b(d)(2).

[36] For a discussion of criticism related to the M.O. and M.C.O. No. 1, see CRS Report RL31600, The Department of Defense Rules for Military Commissions: Analysis of Procedural Rules and Comparison with Proposed Legislation and the Uniform Code of Military Justice, by Jennifer K. Elsea; see *National Institute of Military Justice, Annotated Guide: Procedures for Trials by Military Commissions of Certain Non-United States Citizens in the War Against Terrorism* 10-11(2004)(hereinafter "NIMJ").

[37] M.O. § 1(e) (finding such tribunals necessary to protect the United States and for effective conduct of military operations).

[38] P.L. 107-40, 115 Stat. 224 (2001) (authorizing military force against those who "planned, authorized, committed, [or] aided" the September 11 attacks or who "harbored such ... persons").

[39] See Combatant Status Review Tribunal Procedure, available online at [http://www.defenselink.mil/news/Aug2006/d20060809CSRTProcedures.pdf] (last visited August 13, 2007).

[40] 10 U.S.C. § 948a(1).

[41] See, e.g., Ex parte Milligan, 71 U.S. (4 Wall.) 2 (1866); Duncan v. Kahanamoku, 327 U.S. 304 (1945).

[42] 317 U.S. 1 (1942).

[43] See Department of Defense (DOD) Fact Sheet, "Combatant Status Review Tribunals," available at [http://www.defenselink.mil/news/Jul2004/d20040707factsheet.pdf]. CSRT proceedings are modeled on the procedures of Army Regulation (AR) 190-8, Enemy Prisoners of War, Retained Personnel, Civilian Internees and Other Detainees (1997), which establishes administrative procedures to determine the status of detainees under the Geneva Conventions and prescribes their treatment in accordance with international law. It does not include a category for "unlawful" or "enemy" combatants, who would presumably be covered by the other categories.

[44] See Josh White and Shailagh Murray, Guantanamo Ruling Renews The Debate Over Detainees, *Wash. Post*, June 6, 2007, at A3.

[45] The orders are available on the DOD website at [http://www.defenselink.mil/news/ courtofmilitarycommissionreview.html] (last visited September 14, 2007).

[46] United States v. Khadr, CMCR 07-001 (September 24, 2007), available online at [http://www.defenselink.mil/news/Sep2007/KHADR%20Decision%20(24%20Sep%200 7)(25%20pages).pdf].

[47] Id. at 13.

[48] Id.

[49] Id. at 15 (citing 10 U.S.C. § 948b(f)).

[50] 10 U.S.C. § 948d.

[51] M.C.I. No. 2 was published in draft form by DOD for outside comment. The final version appears to have incorporated some of the revisions, though not all, suggested by those who offered comments. See *National Institute of Military Justice, Military Commission Instructions Sourcebook* 95 (2003) [hereinafter "Sourcebook"].

[52] Crimes against the law of war listed in M.C.I. No. 2 are: 1) Willful Killing of Protected Persons; 2) Attacking Civilians; 3) Attacking Civilian Objects; 4) Attacking Protected Property; 5) Pillaging; 6) Denying Quarter; 7) Taking Hostages; 8) Employing Poison or Analogous Weapons; 9) Using Protected Persons as Shields; 10) Using Protected Property as Shields; 11) Torture; 12) Causing Serious Injury; 13) Mutilation or Maiming; 14) Use of Treachery or Perfidy; 15) Improper Use of Flag of Truce; 16) Improper Use of Protective Emblems; 17) Degrading Treatment of a Dead Body; and 18) Rape.

[53] Crimes "triable by military commissions" include 1) Hijacking or Hazarding a Vessel or Aircraft; 2) Terrorism; 3) Murder by an Unprivileged Belligerent; 4) Destruction of Property by an Unprivileged Belligerent; 5) Aiding the Enemy; 6) Spying; 7) Perjury or False Testimony; and 8) Obstruction of Justice Related to Military Commissions. Listed as "other forms of liability and related offenses" are: 1) Aiding or Abetting; 2) Solicitation; 3) Command/Superior Responsibility - Perpetrating; 4) Command/Superior Responsibility - Misprision; 5) Accessory After the Fact; 6) Conspiracy; and 7) Attempt.

[54] See M.C.I. No. 2 § 3(A) ("No offense is cognizable in a trial by military commission if that offense did not exist prior to the conduct in question.").

[55] For example, Article 3 of the Statute governing the International Criminal Tribunal for the former Yugoslavia (ICTY) includes the following as violations of the laws or customs of war in non-international armed conflict. Such violations shall include, but not be limited to: (a) employment of poisonous weapons or other weapons calculated to cause unnecessary suffering; (b) wanton destruction of cities, towns or villages, or devastation not justified by military necessity; (c) attack, or bombardment, by whatever means, of undefended towns, villages, dwellings, or buildings; (d) seizure of, destruction

or willful damage done to institutions dedicated to religion, charity and education, the arts and sciences, historic monuments and works of art and science; (e) plunder of public or private property. UN Doc. S/Res/827 (1993), art. 3. The ICTY Statute and procedural rules are available at [http://www.un.org/icty/legaldoc-e/index.htm]. The Trial Chamber in the case Prosecutor v. Naletilic and Martinovic, (IT-98-34)March 31, 2003, interpreted Article 3 of the Statute to cover specifically: (i) violations of the Hague law on international conflicts; (ii) infringements of provisions of the Geneva Conventions other than those classified as grave breaches by those Conventions; (iii) violations of [Common Article 3) and other customary rules on internal conflicts, and (iv) violations of agreements binding upon the parties to the conflict" Id. at para. 224. See also Prosecutor v. Tadic, (IT-94-1) (Appeals Chamber), Decision on the Defense Motion for Interlocutory Appeal on Jurisdiction, October 2, 1995, para. 86-89. The Appeals Chamber there set forth factors that make an offense a "serious" violation necessary to bring it within the ICTY's jurisdiction: (i) the violation must constitute an infringement of a rule of international humanitarian law; (ii) the rule must be customary in nature or, if it belongs to treaty law, the required conditions must be met ...; (iii) the violation must be "serious", that is to say, it must constitute a breach of a rule protecting important values, and the breach must involve grave consequences for the victim.... (iv) the violation of the rule must entail, under customary or conventional law, the individual criminal responsibility of the person breaching the rule. Id. at para. 94.

[56] Hamdan v. Rumsfeld, 126 S.Ct. 2749, 2785 (2006).

[57] Prosecutor v. Kvocka et al., Case No. IT-98-30/1 (Trial Chamber), November 2, 2001, para. 124: ("An additional requirement for Common Article 3 crimes under Article 3 of the Statute is that the violations must be committed against persons 'taking no active part in the hostilities.'"); Prosecutor v. Jelisic, Case No. IT-95-10 (Trial Chamber), December 14, 1999, para. 34 ("Common Article 3 protects "[p]ersons taking no active part in the hostilities" including persons "placed hors de combat by sickness, wounds, detention, or any other cause."); Prosecutor v. Blaskic, Case No. IT-95-14 (Trial Chamber), March 3, 2000, para. 180 ("Civilians within the meaning of Article 3 are persons who are not, or no longer, members of the armed forces. Civilian property covers any property that could not be legitimately considered a military objective.").

[58] 10 U.S.C. § 950v(b)(25)(incorporating the definition found in 18 U.S.C. § 2339(A)).

[59] 10 U.S.C. § 950v(b)(13-14). For "serious bodily injury," the MCA specifically includes "lawful combatants" as possible victims.

[60] See Winthrop, supra note 11, at 773 (the law of war "prescribes the rights and obligations of belligerents, or ... define[s] the status and relations not only of

enemies —whether or not in arms — but also of persons under military government or martial law and persons simply resident or being upon the theatre of war, and which authorizes their trial and punishment when offenders"); id at 836 (military commissions have valid jurisdiction only in theater of war or territory under martial law or military government).

[61] Some may argue that no war has a specific deadline and that all conflicts are in a sense indefinite. In traditional armed conflicts, however, it has been relatively easy to identify when hostilities have ended; for example, upon the surrender or annihilation of one party, an annexation of territory under dispute, an armistice or peace treaty, or when one party to the conflict unilaterally withdraws its forces. See Gerhard Von Glahn, *Law Among Nations* 722-730 (6th ed. 1992).

[62] See Human Rights First, Trial Under Military Order, A Guide to the Final Rules for Military Commissions (revised May 2006)[hereinafter "HRF"], available at [http://www.humanrightsfirst.org/us_law/PDF/detainees/trials_ under_order0604.pdf]] (last visited August 13, 2007); See Leila Nadya Sadat, Terrorism and the Rule of Law, 3 WASH. U. GLOBAL STUD. L. REV. 135, 146 (2004) (noting possibly advantageous domestic aspects of treating terrorist attacks as war crimes, but identifying possible pitfalls of creating a new international legal regime).

[63] 10 U.S.C. § 948d.

[64] M.C.I. No. 2 § 5(C).

[65] Id.

[66] See Sourcebook, supra note 51, at 38-39 (NACDL comments); id. at 51 (Human Rights Watch (HRW) comments); id. at 59-60 (LCHR). However, M.C.I. No. 9 lists among possible "material errors of law" for which the Reviewing Panel might return a finding for further procedures, "a conviction of a charge that fails to state an offense that by statute or the law of war may be tried by military commission...." M.C.I. No. 9 § 4(C)(2)(b).

[67] See Sourcebook, supra note 51, at 38 (NACDL comments).

[68] See id. at 98 (commentary of Eugene R. Fidell and Michael F. Noone).

[69] M.C.O. No. 1 § 4(A)(3).

[70] See 10 U.S.C. § 603, listed as reference (e) of M.C.O. No. 1.

[71] M.C.O. No. 1 § 4(A)(4). See *NIMJ*, supra note 36, at 17 (commenting that the lack of a military judge to preside over the proceedings is a significant departure from the UCMJ). A judge advocate is a military officer of the Judge Advocate General's Corps of the Army or Navy (a military lawyer). A military judge is a judge advocate who is certified as qualified by the JAG Corps of his or her service to serve in a role similar to civilian judges.

[72] 10 U.S.C. §§ 948m and 949m.

[73] See M.C.O. No. 1 § 3(C) (asserting jurisdiction over participants in commission proceedings "as necessary to preserve the integrity and order of the proceedings").
[74] Rule for Military Commissions (R.M.C.) 809.
[75] See 10 U.S.C. § 848. This section is made inapplicable to military commissions in chapter 47a by MCA § 4.
[76] 10 U.S.C. § 950j.
[77] R.M.C. 703.
[78] See 10 U.S.C. § 847. It is unclear how witnesses are "duly subpoenaed;" 10 U.S.C. § 846 empowers the president of the court-martial to compel witnesses to appear and testify and to compel production of evidence, but this statutory authority does not explicitly apply to military commissions. The subpoena power extends to "any part of the United States, or the Territories, Commonwealth and possessions."
[79] R.M.C. 703; R.C.M. 703.
[80] Hamdan, slip op. at 11-16 (Kennedy, J. concurring).
[81] See 10 U.S.C. § 836 (providing military commission rules "may not be contrary to or inconsistent with [the UCMJ]"). But see In re Yamashita, 327 U.S. 1, 19-20 (1946)(finding Congress did not intend the language "military commission" in Article 38 of the Articles of War, the precursor to UCMJ Art. 36, to mean military commissions trying enemy combatants). President Bush explicitly invoked UCMJ art. 36 as statutory authority for the M.O., and included a finding, "consistent with section 836 of title 10, United States Code, that it is not practicable to apply in military commissions under this order the principles of law and the rules of evidence generally recognized in the trial of criminal cases in the United States district courts." M.O. § 1(g). The Supreme Court, however, rejected that finding as unsupported by the record and read the "uniformity" clause of UCMJ art. 36 as requiring that military commissions must follow rules as close as possible to those that apply in courts-martial.
[82] M.C.O. No. 1 § 1.
[83] Id. § 10.
[84] Id.; M.C.I. No. 1 § 6 (Non-Creation of Right).
[85] M.C.O. No. 1 § 5(A).
[86] 10 U.S.C. § 948q.
[87] M.C.O. No. 1 §§ 5(B) and 6(B); 10 U.S.C. § 949i.
[88] 10 U.S.C. § 949a(b).
[89] Id. §§ 4(A)(5)(a); 5(K); 6B(3).
[90] M.C.O. No. 1 § 6(D)(5).
[91] M.C.O. No. 1 at § 6(B)(3)("Open proceedings may include, at the discretion of the Appointing Authority, attendance by the public and accredited press, and public release of transcripts at the appropriate time."). In courts-martial,

"public" is defined to include members of the military as well as civilian communities. Rules for Court-Martial (R.C.M.) Rule 806.
[92] See Globe Newspaper Co. v. Super. Ct., 457 U.S. 596, 602 (1982)(newspaper had standing to challenge court order closing portions of criminal trial).
[93] United States v. Hershey, 20 M.J. 433 (C.M.A.1985), cert. denied, 474 U.S. 1062 (1986); United States v. Grunden, 2 M.J. 116 (C.M.A.1977). The press has standing to challenge closure of military justice proceedings. ABC, Inc. v. Powell, 47 M.J. 363, 365 (1997).
[94] See Press-Enterprise Co. v. Superior Court of California, 464 U.S. 501 (1984).
[95] 10 U.S.C. § 949d(d).
[96] Pell v. Procunier, 417 U.S. 817, 822-24 (1974).
[97] See Juan R. Torruella, On the Slippery Slopes of Afghanistan: Military Commissions and the Exercise of Presidential Power, 4 *U. Pa. J. Const. L.* 648, 718 (2002) (noting that proceedings held at the Guantánamo Bay Naval Station may be de facto closed due to the physical isolation of the facility).
[98] Cf. Detroit Free Press v. Ashcroft, 303 F.3d 681 (6th Cir. 2002) (finding closure of immigration hearings based on relation to events of September 11 unconstitutional infringement on the First Amendment right to free press). But see North Jersey Media Group, Inc. v. Ashcroft, 308 F.3d 198 (3d Cir. 2002) cert denied 538 U.S. 1056 (2003)(no presumption of openness for immigration hearings).
[99] 10 U.S.C. § 839.
[100] 10 U.S.C. § 949d(e).
[101] 10 U.S.C. § 948k.
[102] 10 U.S.C. § 949c(b); R.M.C. 804.
[103] 10 U.S.C. § 949a(b)(2)(D). M.C.I. No. 4 required detailed defense counsel to "defend the accused zealously within the bounds of the law ... notwithstanding any intention expressed by the accused to represent himself." M.C.I. No. 4 § 3(C).
[104] M.C.O. No. 1 § 4(C). M.C.I. No. 4 § 3(D) listed criteria for the "availability" of selected detailed counsel.
[105] Regulation for Trial by Military Commissions, Para. 9-2. The accused may request a specific JAG officer from the cadre of officers assigned to the Defense Counsel's Office, but does not have a right to choose.
[106] 10 U.S.C. § 949c(b)(5).
[107] R.M.C. 501.
[108] R.M.C. 506(c).
[109] 10 U.S.C. § 949c(b).
[110] Originally, civilian attorneys were required to pay the costs associated with obtaining a clearance. M.C.I. No. 5 §3(A)(2)(d)(ii). DOD later waived the administrative costs for processing applications for TOP SECRET clearances in

cases that would require the higher level of security clearance. See DOD Press Release No. 084-04 , New Military Commission Orders, Annex Issued (February 6, 2004), available at [http://www.defenselink.mil/releases/2004/nr20040206-0331.html] (Last visited August 15, 2007).
[111] M.C.O. No. 1 § 4(C)(3)(b).
[112] 10 U.S.C. §949c, R.M.C. 502(d)(3).
[113] M.C.I. No. 5 § 3(e)(B)(6).
[114] Regulation for Trial by Military Commissions, Para. 9-5(c).
[115] Mil. R. Evid. 502.
[116] See M.C.O. No. 3, "Special Administrative Measures for Certain Communications Subject to Monitoring." The required affidavit and agreement annexed to M.C.I. No. 3 was modified to eliminate the following language: I understand that my communications with my client, even if traditionally covered by the attorney-client privilege, may be subject to monitoring or review by government officials, using any available means, for security and intelligence purposes. I understand that any such monitoring will only take place in limited circumstances when approved by proper authority, and that any evidence or information derived from such communications will not be used in proceedings against the Accused who made or received the relevant communication.
[117] M.C.I. No. 5, Annex B § II(J).
[118] Regulation for Trial by Military Commissions, Figure 9.2. Affidavit and Agreement by Civilian Defense Counsel, II(J).
[119] U.S. CONST. Amdt. VI applies in courts-martial. E.g. United States v. Scheffer, 523 U.S. 303 (1998).
[120] Maryland v. Craig, 497 U.S. 836, 845 (1990).
[121] The Military Rules of Evidence (Mil. R. Evid.) are contained in the Manual for Courts-Martial (M.C.M.), established as Exec. Order No. 12473, Manual for Courts-Martial, United States, 49 Fed. Reg 17,152, (April 23, 1984), as amended. The M.C.M. also contains the procedural rules for courts-martial, known as the Rules For Courts-Martial (R.C.M.).
[122] Mil. R. Evid. 402.
[123] Mil. R. Evid. 403 (relevant evidence may be excluded "if its probative value is substantially outweighed by the danger of unfair prejudice, confusion of the issues, or misleading the members, or by considerations of undue delay, waste of time, or needless presentation of cumulative evidence").
[124] See R.C.M. 701(a)(6); *NIMJ*, supra note 36, at 31-32.
[125] Mil. R. Evid. 505 provides procedures similar to the Classified Information Protection Act (CIPA) that applies in civilian court.
[126] Hamdan v. Rumsfeld, 126 S.Ct. 2749, 2798 (2006)(while accepting that the government "has a compelling interest in denying [the accused] access to

certain sensitive information," stating that "at least absent express statutory provision to the contrary, information used to convict a person of a crime must be disclosed to him").

[127] 10 U.S.C. § 949a.

[128] 10 U.S.C. § 949j.

[129] M.C.O. No. 1, § 5(E) (requiring such information, as well as any exculpatory evidence known by the prosecution, to be provided to the accused as long as such information was not deemed to be protected under Sec. 6(D)(5)).

[130] 10 U.S.C. § 949j.

[131] M.C.O. No. 1, § 6 (defining "Protected Information" to include classified or classifiable information, information protected "by law or rule from unauthorized disclosure," information that could endanger trial participants, intelligence and law enforcement sources, methods or activities, or "information concerning other national security interests").

[132] M.C.O. No. 1, § 6(D)(5)(b). Some observers noted that protected information could include exculpatory evidence as well as incriminating evidence, which could implicate 6th Amendment rights and rights under the Geneva Convention, if applicable. See HRF, supra note 62, at 3.

[133] M.C.O. No. 1 § 6(D)(5)(b).

[134] It is not clear what information would be required to be provided under this subsection. Discovery at court-martial is controlled by R.C.M. 701, which requires trial counsel to provide to the defense any papers accompanying the charges, sworn statements in the possession of trial counsel that relate to the charges, and all documents and tangible objects within the possession or control of military authorities that are material to the preparation of the defense or that are intended for use in the prosecution's case-in-chief at trial. Exculpatory evidence is not defined, but it appears to be encompassed under "evidence favorable to the defense," which includes evidence that tends to negate the guilt of the accused of an offense charged, reduce the degree of guilt, or reduce the applicable punishment. The M.M.C. defines "exculpatory evidence" in those same terms. R.M.C. 701(e).

[135] R.M.C. 701(f)(3).

[136] 10 U.S.C. § 949j.

[137] R.M.C. 701(f)(5). Protective orders are covered under Mil. Comm. R. Evid. 505, and include orders that limit the scope of direct examination and cross examination of witnesses.

[138] R.M.C. 701(f)(2).

[139] Mil. Comm. R. Evid. 505(e)(4).

[140] Id. The corresponding rule for courts-martial, Mil. R. Evid. 505, provides that the military judge, upon finding that the lack of production of information

would materially prejudice a substantial right of the accused, must "dismiss the charges or specifications or both to which the classified information relates."
[141] M.C.O. No. 1 § 6(D)(1). At courts-martial, evidence is admitted if it is "relevant," meaning "tending to make the existence of any fact that is of consequence to the determination of the action more probable or less probable than it would be without the evidence." Mil. R. Evid. 401. At military commissions, evidence meets the standard of "probative to a reasonable person" if "a reasonable person would regard the evidence as making the existence of any fact that is of consequence to a determination of the commission action more probable or less probable than it would be without the evidence." Mil. Comm. R. Evid. 403.
[142] 10 U.S.C. § 949a(b)(2)(F); Mil. Comm. R. Evid. 403.
[143] Mil. Com. R. Evid. 304(d).
[144] Mil. Com. R. Evid. 304(f).
[145] Mil. R. Evid. 801-807 provide procedures for determining the admissibility of hearsay evidence in courts-martial. It is unclear how, under the MCA, it is to be determined whether certain hearsay evidence would be admissible in a general court-martial.
[146] 10 U.S.C. § 949a(b)(3)).
[147] See Jencks v. United States, 353 U.S. 657 (1957)("Requiring the accused first to show conflict between the reports [in the possession of the government] and the testimony is actually to deny the accused evidence relevant and material to his defense.").
[148] Mil. R. Evid. 803 (exceptions for which the availability of the declarant is immaterial); Mil. R. Evid. 804 (exceptions applicable when declarant is unavailable); Mil. R. Evid. 807 (residual exception, which permits all other hearsay not covered by express exceptions when there are "equivalent circumstantial guarantees of trustworthiness" and the military judge determines the statement relates to a material fact, is more probative to that fact than other reasonably obtainable evidence, and that its introduction into evidence "serves the general purposes of the rules and the interest of justice").
[149] Mil. Comm. R. Evid. 803(b)(2).
[150] Mil. Comm. R. Evid. 803(c).
[151] Defined in 10 U.S.C. §948a(4) as "[a]ny information or material that has been determined by the United States Government pursuant to statute, Executive order, or regulation to require protection against unauthorized disclosure for reasons of national security" and "restricted data, as that term is defined in section 11y of the Atomic Energy Act of 1954 (42 U.S.C. 2014(y))."
[152] 10 U.S.C. § 949d(f)(3).
[153] Cf. Crane v. Kentucky, 476 U.S. 683 (1986)(evidence about the manner in which a confession was obtained should have been admitted as relevant to its

reliability and credibility despite court's determination that the confession was voluntary and need not be suppressed).

[154] Cf. Ohio v. Roberts, 448 U.S. 56, 66 (1980)(admissibility of hearsay evidence), but cf. Crawford v. Washington, 541 U.S. 36 (2004)("Admitting statements deemed reliable by a judge is fundamentally at odds with the right of confrontation.... [The Confrontation Clause] commands ... that reliability be assessed in a particular manner: by testing in the crucible of cross-examination.").

[155] M.M.C. at III-26.

[156] Mil. Comm. R. Evid. 505(f). Similar procedures are permitted courts-martial. Mil. R. Evid. 505(j).

[157] Mil. Comm. R. Evid. 505(g). This rule is virtually identical to Mil. R. Evid. 505(h).

[158] See *NIMJ*, supra note 36, at 37 (citing United States v. Rosato, 32 M.J. 93, 96 (C.M.A. 1991)).

[159] The method of execution used by the Army to carry out a death sentence by military commission is lethal injection. See U.S. Army Correctional System: Procedures for Military Executions, AR 190-55 (1999). It is unclear whether DOD will follow these regulations with respect to sentences issued by these military commissions, but it appears unlikely that any such sentences would be carried out at Ft. Leavenworth, in accordance with AR 190-55.

[160] M.C.I. No. 7 § 3(A).

[161] M.C.O. No. 1 § 6(F).

[162] 10 U.S.C. § 851.

[163] 10 U.S.C. § 948d.

[164] 10 U.S.C. § 949s.

[165] The MCA permits the death penalty for convictions of murder of a protected person or murder in violation of the law of war, or spying; and if death results, any of the following crimes: attacking civilians, taking hostages, employing poison or similar weapon, using protected persons as a shield, torture or cruel or inhuman treatment, intentionally causing serious bodily injury, maiming, using treachery or perfidy, hijacking or hazarding a vessel or aircraft, terrorism, and conspiracy to commit any of the crimes enumerated in 10 U.S.C. § 950v.

[166] 10 U.S.C. § 949m.

[167] An accused sentenced to death may neither waive his right to appeal nor withdraw an appeal. 10 U.S.C. § 950c.

[168] R.M.C. 1001(b)(2). Otherwise, aggravating factors are similar to those listed in R.C.M. 1001(b)(5)(D) for courts-martial.

[169] R.M.C. 1001(c)(2)(D). The trial counsel may rebut the statement. This procedure does not appear to differ substantially from that used in courts-martial.

[170] R.M.C. 1004(c).

[171] Persons subject to the M.O. were described as not privileged to "seek any remedy or maintain any proceeding, directly or indirectly" in federal or state court, the court of any foreign nation, or any international tribunal. M.O. at § 7(b). However, the Administration originally indicated that defendants were permitted to petition a federal court for a writ of habeas corpus to challenge the jurisdiction of the military commission. See Alberto R. Gonzales, Martial Justice, Full and Fair, *New York Times* (op-ed), November 30, 2001 (stating that the original M.O. was not intended to preclude habeas corpus review). Rasul v. Bush clarified that the detainees at Guantanamo Bay do have access to federal courts, but the extent to which the findings of military commissions will be reviewable was not clarified. 124 S. Ct. 2686 (2004). Congress, by enacting the DTA and the MCA, has revoked the jurisdiction of federal courts over habeas corpus petitions filed by or on behalf of aliens detained by the United States as enemy combatants. For an analysis of the habeas provisions in these Acts, see CRS Report RL33180, Enemy Combatant Detainees: Habeas Corpus Challenges in Federal Court, by Jennifer K. Elsea and Kenneth Thomas.

[172] See Laurence H. Tribe, Trial by Fury, *The New Republic*, December 10, 2001.

[173] The convening authority of a general court-martial is required to consider all matters presented by the accused. 10 U.S.C. § 860. The MCA contains a similar provision. 10 U.S.C. § 950b.

[174] M.C.I. No. 9 § 4(C).

[175] 10 U.S.C. § 8037 (listing among duties of Air Force Judge Advocate General to "receive, revise, and have recorded the proceedings of ... military commissions"); 10 U.S.C. § 3037 (similar duty ascribed to Army Judge Advocate General).

[176] 10 U.S.C. § 950f.

[177] 10 U.S.C. § 950g. No collateral attack on the verdict is permitted. 10 U.S.C. § 949j(b) provides that Except as otherwise provided in this chapter and notwithstanding any other provision of law (including section 2241 of title 28 or any other habeas corpus provision), no court, justice, or judge shall have jurisdiction to hear or consider any claim or cause of action whatsoever, including any action pending on or filed after the date of the enactment of the Military Commissions Act of 2006, relating to the prosecution, trial, or judgment of a military commission under this chapter, including challenges to the lawfulness of procedures of military commissions under this chapter.

[178] 10 U.S.C. § 950g.

[179] 10 U.S.C. § 859; 10 U.S.C. § 950a(a).

[180] M.C.I. No. 9 § 4(C)(2)(a).

[181] M.C.I. No. 9 § 4(C)(1)(b).

[182] R.M.C. 1102(b).
[183] R.M.C. 1105.
[184] R.M.C. 1106.
[185] R.M.C. 1107.
[186] R.M.C. 1102A.
[187] R.M.C. 1107(e).
[188] R.M.C. 1107(f)(5).
[189] R.M.C. 1111. Courts-martial findings are first forwarded to the Judge Advocate General of the particular service for legal review, R.C.M. 1112.
[190] R.M.C. 1201.
[191] R.M.C. 1210.
[192] M.C.O. No. 1 § 5(P). The finding was to become final when "the President or, if designated by the President, the Secretary of Defense makes a final decision thereon pursuant to Section 4(c)(8) of the President's Military Order and in accordance with Section 6(H)(6) of [M.C.O. No. 1]." Id. § 6(H)(2).
[193] 10 U.S.C. § 844. Federal courts and U.S. military courts are considered to serve under the same sovereign for purposes of double (or former) jeopardy.
[194] In regular courts-martial, the record of a proceeding is "authenticated," or certified as to its accuracy, by the military judge who presided over the proceeding. R.C.M. 1104. None of the military orders or instructions establishing procedures for military commissions explains what is meant by "authenticated finding."
[195] M.C.O. No. 1 § 6(H)(2).
[196] The UCMJ does not permit rehearing on a charge for which the accused is found on the facts to be not guilty.
[197] 10 U.S.C. § 949h.
[198] 10 U.S.C. § 950b(d)(2)(B).
[199] R.M.C. 1102(c).
[200] Id. At courts-martial, sessions to increase the severity of a sentence are permitted only if the sentence is mandatory. R.C.M. 1102(c).
[201] See M.C.O. No. 1 § 6(A)(1).
[202] See NIMJ, supra note 36, at 39.
[203] 10 U.S.C. § 948q.
[204] 10 U.S.C. § 948s.
[205] R.M.C. 307.
[206] Id.
[207] R.C.M. 602.
[208] R.C.M. 602.
[209] M.O. § 7(e).

[210] R.M.C. 907.

INDEX

D

E

J

K

L

M

N

T

U

V

W

Y